Teacher Study Guide

for

If I Should Speak

Saba Negash

Al-Walaa Publications

© 2012 Al-Walaa Publications All Rights Reserved
Teacher Study Guide for If I Should Speak

The classroom teacher may reproduce copies of materials in this book for classroom use only. The reproduction of any part for an entire school or school system is strictly prohibited. No part of this publication may be transmitted, stored or recorded in any form without the written permission of the publisher.

Al-Walaa Publications
College Park, MD
USA

ISBN 978-0-9707667-7-9

Teacher Study Guide authored by Saba Negash
Content Development by Linda D. Delgado
Book Design by Leila Joiner

Printed in the United States of America

Table of Contents

Introduction 4

Chapter One 5
Chapter Two 11
Chapter Three 16
Chapter Four 22
Chapter Five 27
Chapter Six 34
Chapter Seven 39
Chapter Eight 44
Chapter Nine 50
Chapter Ten 56
Chapter Eleven 61
Chapter Twelve 66
Chapter Thirteen 70
Chapter Fourteen 77
Chapter Fifteen 83

Teacher Tool Kit 89

    A. Book Characters' Descriptions 90
    B. Reference List 91
    C. Arabic-English Glossary 92
    D. A Quick Grammar Review 94
    E. Islamic Fiction Definition and Fiction Writing Review 96
    F. Recommended Reading List 98
    G. Level I Book Review Guide 99
    H. Level II Book Review Guide 100
    I. Answer Key – Level I and II 102

Introduction

The Teacher Study Guide (TSG) is designed to be a valuable support tool for Islamic school teachers and homeschooling parents with students having different levels of critical thinking, reading comprehension, and creative writing skills.

The content of the TSG was developed for Level I: seventh and eighth graders and ESL students and Level II: high school and young adult students. The TSG is designed to allow the teacher to choose which assignments and discussion topics will be introduced to students.

Each chapter includes discussion topics and talking points related to the topics, vocabulary words and usage, and student assignments to strengthen their reading and writing skills.

Vocabulary:

A vocabulary word list is included in a side bar on the first page of each new chapter. Level I students should be assigned to write the definition for each word and use the correct word in sentences provided in the TSG. Level II students should be required to write each word's definition and write a sentence using each vocabulary word correctly. A Quick Grammar Review is located in the Teacher Tool Kit.

The teacher can also choose to create crossword and/or seek 'n find puzzles for students using the vocabulary words provided in each chapter. A puzzle maker tool is available on the internet at: http://www.puzzle-maker.com/CW/

Writing Assignments:

It is recommended that on the first day of class the teacher assign students to keep a journal and write their thoughts about what they read in each chapter. It is suggested that, on a regular basis, the teacher asks a few of the students to read one of their journal entries.

The TSG includes two writing assignments, one Islamic fiction short story assignment, essay Q&A in each chapter, journal writing, and at the conclusion of the book a written book review assignment.

It is recommended that the teacher establish a standard format for essay assignments and the Islamic fiction story students will be required to write. A recommended format is as follows: Times New Roman font style, 12 point font size, ½ paragraph indents, one inch margins, either single or double-spaced lines, and a minimum and maximum word count for essays and the Islamic fiction story.

Chapter One

1. **Teacher provides the story setting description:**
   - Location: Streamsdale, Georgia – Streamsdale University, co-educational, on campus dorm rooms and apartments.
   - Second semester of Tamika's sophomore year at the university. Tamika is sharing a dorm room with one other female student.

2. **Discussion:** Ask students to describe the book characters introduced in Chapter One and use a white board to write down students' answers. *Refer to Teacher Tool Kit (A).

3. **Discussion:** Fight in the Dorm Room. Ask several students to describe the fight. Use a white board to record their responses.

   ### Talking Points:
   - Jennifer's injuries: She bumped her head causing a small cut that did not require stitches.
   - Jennifer attacked Tamika after calling her obscenities and a terrible name considered a racial slur.
   - Tamika's injuries: Thin red welts swelled across her cheeks, the result of Jennifer's irate fingernails scraping her skin; their presence should have suggested that she had been a victim.
   - Tamika's actions were defensive to keep Jennifer from hitting and scratching her more.
   - Tamika was charged with physical assault and ordered to attend a Conduct Board Hearing at Streamsdale University Student Center at 6:45 the next evening.

4. **Discussion:** Summarize the Conduct Board Hearing and what Jennifer did or did not do to represent or defend herself.

   ### Talking Points:
   - Jennifer testified that she felt unsafe around Tamika because of Tamika's alleged prior intimidation and the feeling that at any moment Tamika would become violent.
   - Jennifer exaggerated Tamika's part in the fight and covered up her own violent behavior and her racial attack on Tamika.
   - Jennifer had witnesses testify on her behalf even though none had witnessed the fight.

5. **Discussion:** What was Tamika's attitude about the fight and the Conduct Hearing?

   ### Talking Points:
   - Tamika chose to attend the Conduct Board Hearing without a Faculty Advisor, who could act somewhat like a lawyer for her.

Vocabulary:
Dormitory
Strenuous
Advisor
Exaggerate
Collateral
Expound
Testimony
Articulate
Feigned
Villain
Irate
Irrefutable
Isolated

- The entire hearing was a joke to Tamika, and the idea of a "lawyer" seemed ludicrous in light of the trivial altercation with her roommate."
- She thought who on her earth could testify on her behalf. Besides, who had actually witnessed the incident?
- Even after learning the seriousness of the charge against her, Tamika barely paid any attention to Jennifer and the witnesses who testified at the hearing.
- Tamika felt overwhelmed.
- She realized too late the need for a Faculty Advisor.
- She felt isolated and alone as she was painted a villain.
- The room harbored an unfriendly atmosphere that she could not break.
- She imagined that it would not matter what she said at that point, and she was certain that she had lost the case.
- She tuned out their testimony and daydreamed about her first meeting with Dr. Sanders when she took his Religion 101 course the year before.
- Because Dr. Sanders was a member of the Conduct Board she thought he would be sympathetic and believe her because he was also African-American.

6. **Discussion:** What things could Tamika have done to help herself, but didn't, prior to her Conduct Hearing?

   Talking Points for before the fight between Jennifer and Tamika:
   - Tamika could have reported Jennifer for failing to help with the housekeeping tasks of keeping the dorm room clean.
   - Tamika could have reported Jennifer for making telephone calls to her mother and telling her mother lies about Tamika.
   - Tamika could have requested a change in her dorm room assignment or requested Jennifer be moved.
   - After the fight Tamika could have told the security officers and Mandy the resident advisor, about the racial slur and showed them the scratch marks across her face to prove Jennifer had attacked her and support what she said about keeping Jennifer's hands away from her.
   - Tamika could have prayed.
   - She could have contacted her best friend Makisha for support and to testify as to her knowledge of Tamika's non-violent conduct.
   - She could have contacted her family for advice and support.
   - She could have filed a complaint against Jennifer for assault and or for racial discrimination.

7. **Discussion:** Did Tamika's behavior during the Conduct Hearing help or hurt her believability? Ask the students to explain their answers.

8. **Discussion:** The Conduct Board found Tamika guilty. She was ordered to move out of the room she had shared with Jennifer and the physical assault charge and guilty finding were made part of her college record. What was her reaction?

Talking Points:
– Tamika was angry with the Conduct Board members, especially Dr. Sanders.
– Tamika blamed "the injustice of the so-called "justice" system of America.
– Tamika had a false assumption that Dr. Sanders did nothing to defend or help her.
– Tamika realized only after it was too late to help herself that her failure to take the Conduct Hearing seriously and prepare a defense for herself impacted the opinion of the students on the conduct hearing.

9. **Discussion:** Tamika cited many reasons why the Conduct Board voted her guilty. How did Tamika's own behavior contribute to the Board's opinion of Tamika?

Talking Points:
– Tamika did not file any complaints against Jennifer.
– She did not request a Faculty Advisor, who could act somewhat like a lawyer for her.
– She walked into the hearing room smiling and waving, acting like the hearing wasn't a serious matter to her.
– She didn't pay attention to the testimony and a student board member had to get her attention focused on the hearing.
– A student on the Board had to prompt her to testify and they had to ask questions rather than Tamika giving a planned defense of what had happened.
– She gave the impression that she did not respect the board hearing process or student members.

10. **Discussion:** Friday, the day after the Board Hearing, Tamika didn't attend her classes. Tamika's Christian friend, Makisha, finds out what happened and scolds Tamika for not going to classes. After Makisha leaves Tamika begins to cry and feels over-whelmed. Tamika reflects on her life.

Talking Points:
– She had not declared a major yet.
– Tamika never wanted to go to college in the first place, desiring to pursue a career in the music industry as a recording artist.
– She had been forced to take high level science and mathematics courses, which were required for graduation, and she was lost.
– She was too shy to ask questions for fear people would think she was stupid.
– She was tired of seeking to prove the world wrong on things they would believe no matter what she did.
– Her mother, other family, and friends were cheering her on, encouraging her to be the person they were unable to be—even if she did not want to be that person, and even if she was not cut out to be that person.
– She did not feel like fighting the battles of the workplace, with its pervasive racism and sexism. The new workers often became her manager although they were not even employed when she began working there.

11. **Discussion:** How did Tamika find comfort after the hearing?

Talking Points:

– Paper and pen were dearer to her than gold at those moments. The lyrics would come to her, and she would frantically write, hoping the words did not escape her mind before the pen could catch them.

– She felt that her poetry and songs were as good as anybody's, if not better, so why couldn't she make it like others had? The words had not escaped her mind before she was able to write them down, and for that, Tamika was grateful. It was short, she knew, but sometimes that was enough, especially for journal entries, which she wrote whenever she felt like it.

12. **Discussion:** Ask students what they thought of Tamika's poem.

Vocabulary List:

1. Dormitory - *noun* a college or university building containing living quarters for students; a large sleeping room containing several beds
2. Strenuous - *adj.* characterized by or performed with much energy or force; taxing to the utmost; testing powers of endurance
3. Advisor - *noun* an expert who gives advice
4. Exaggerate - *verb* to enlarge beyond bounds or the truth; do something to an excessive degree
5. Collateral - *adj.* descended from a common ancestor but through different lines; situated or running side-by-side
6. Expound - *verb* add details, as to an account or idea; clarify the meaning of and discourse in a learned way, usually in writing; state
7. Testimony – *noun* something that serves as evidence; an assertion offering firsthand authentication of a fact
8. Articulate - *adj.* expressing yourself easily or characterized by clear expressive language
9. Feigned - *adj.* not genuine
10. Villain - *noun* a wicked or evil person; someone who does evil deliberately; the principle bad character in a film or work of fiction
11. Irate - *adj.* feeling or showing extreme anger
12. Irrefutable - *adj.* impossible to deny or disprove
13. Isolated - *adj.* not close together in time; having minimal contact or little in common with others

Level I Quiz

1. Tamika was upset with Jennifer because:
   (a) Jennifer refused to help keep the dorm room clean
   (b) Jennifer told her mother lies about Tamika
   (c) Jennifer called Tamika a horrible name considered a racial slur
   (d) All of the above

2. Tamika didn't show the security her injury from Jennifer's nails. What was her injury?
   (a) Red welts across her face from Jennifer's finger nails
   (b) Broken fingernails
   (c) A bruise on right arm
   (d) None of the above

3. What was Tamika's attitude about the Conduct Board Hearing before she went to it?
   (a) The entire hearing was a joke to Tamika.
   (b) She thought it was a trivial altercation with her roommate.
   (c) She thought who on her earth could testify on her behalf as no one saw the fight.
   (d) All of the above

4. Tamika's conduct at the Conduct Board Hearing reflected negatively on her. What did Tamika do or not do that gave a poor impression?
   (a) She walked into the hearing room smiling and waving; acting like the hearing wasn't a serious matter to her.
   (b) Tamika didn't pay attention to Jennifer and the witnesses who testified at the hearing.
   (c) She did not request a Faculty Advisor.
   (d) All of the above

5. After Tamika was found guilty she was upset with Dr. Sanders. Why?
   (a) She thought he should have voted for her because they were both African American.
   (b) He should have volunteered to be a witness for her.
   (c) He was unfriendly to her.
   (d) None of the above

True or False (for false statements allow students to discuss the correct answer)

1. Tamika was excited about moving to the new apartment. (T or F)
2. Tamika had always wanted to attend university. (T or F)
3. Tamika loved to write poetry and create songs from the poetry. (T or F)
4. Tamika felt the Conduct Board students discriminated against her because of her race. (T or F)
5. Tamika was embarrassed to attend her religion class because she had not chosen a topic for her required paper and because Dr. Sanders was a member of the Conduct Board. (T or F)

Level II Essay Questions

1. Why did what happened to Tamika in Chapter One become a good thing? Explain.
2. Tamika is shown in Chapter One to be ambivalent about her religious beliefs and also about her attendance at the university. Explain.
3. What do you think the author meant when she wrote "….the injustice of the so-called "justice" system of America."
4. Tamika has a pattern of behavior that often has negative consequences for her. Please explain.
5. The author does not include the word that is the racial slur against Tamika. Do you think she should have spelled out the word? Explain your answer.

Chapter Two

1. **Teacher provides the story setting in Chapter Two:**
   – First day back in Dr. Sander's class after her guilty verdict.
   – The Conduct Board's closed door discussion on how to punish Tamika.
   – Tamika moves into her new place in Steward Hall University apartment.

2. **Discussion:** Ask students to describe the book characters introduced in Chapter Two and use a white board to write down students' answers. *Refer to Teacher Tool Kit (A).

3. **Discussion:** Explain Tamika's feeling of sadness that she has to leave her dorm room despite the fact that she is not really attached to the room itself neither does she want to live with Jennifer anymore.

   Talking Points:
   – Tamika does not want to live in Steward Hall.
   – Tamika is not looking forward to sharing a space with three roommates.
   – Tamika does not feel her punishment is fair for what really happened.

4. **Discussion:** Tamika is not thrilled to return back to her classes after her ordeal but she is even less thrilled about the repercussions of NOT attending her classes. What are some of the repercussions?

   Talking Points:
   – Falling behind in her course work
   – Failing grades
   – Leaving school
   – Returning home to her mother who would not let her live down her failure

5. **Discussion:** Dr. Sanders considers Tamika to be one of his favorite students. What makes Tamika stand out from the other students?

   Talking Points:
   – Tamika was talkative and friendly.
   – Tamika reminded him of his own daughter.
   – She smiled and laughed a lot.
   – Tamika was sincere and pure; didn't belong to the 'liberal' 'carefree' student body
   – Peaceful composure; calm nature not conducive to violence.

| Repercussions |
| Assault |
| Skeptical |
| Stereotype |
| Influx |
| Expel |
| Altercation |
| Verdict |
| Prejudice |
| Motive |
| Bias |
| Judgmental |
| Controversial |
| Khimar |
| Wudhu |
| Ablution |

6. **Discussion:** Bias and Prejudice

   Talking Points:
   - What does prejudice mean? What does bias mean?
   - How did prejudice and bias affect the decision of the Conduct Board?
   - Do you think people in general are biased or prejudiced towards others? Why?
   - Is it possible to be biased without being prejudiced or vice versa?
   - What about Tamika when she learns that her roommates are Muslim? Is she biased in her way of thinking or prejudiced towards Muslims? Why?
   - What are some ways we can remove racial and religious bias and prejudice from our society?

7. **Discussion:** Dr. Sanders is convinced bias and prejudice played a big role in the Conduct Board's decision to convict Tamika of 'Physical Assault.'

   Talking Points:
   - Tamika has no prior record but they want to expel her.
   - Students with worse and repeated offences were not expelled.
   - The board's disinterest in Jennifer's part that led to the fight.
   - The board exaggerating Jennifer's injuries to make Tamika seem dangerous by stating she 'busted' Jennifer's head.

8. **Discussion:** The Conduct Board, mainly Jonathan and Sarah, think Tamika poses a "clear and present danger" to the student body even though she has no prior record to the incident with Jennifer. Michael and the remaining members believe she poses only a threat to Jennifer.

   Talking Points:
   - Stereotypes: All blacks are prone to being violent, dangerous, criminals etc.
   - Prejudice: Sarah and Jonathan refuse to admit the altercation was a fight between Jennifer and Tamika as opposed to a vicious attack by Tamika.
   - Prejudice: The board ignored Jennifer's role in the fight as well, sighting Tamika as the only offender despite the fact that Jennifer started the fight.
   - Bias: Michael and the rest of the Board were willing to assume that because Tamika fought back she might be a further threat to Jennifer.
   - Bias: The security officers and Conduct Board were more concerned with Jennifer's superficial injuries and showed no interest in Tamika's injuries from the altercation.

9. **Discussion:** Tamika is unsure how she feels about living with Muslims, namely Aminah. She is even more confused when she learns Dee is a Muslim too.

   Talking Points:
   - She's not sure if she will get along with her roommates.
   - Living with Muslims will be stressful.
   - She thinks Muslims are strict and judgmental.

10. **Discussion:** Despite their friendship, Aminah is unsure about living with Dee/Durrah and finds it stressful. She would rather live in her own apartment but their mothers insist upon them living together. At the same time, Aminah keeps many of Dee's un-Islamic behavior a secret from their parents.

Talking Points:

– Dee takes the religion lightly; ex: she makes a joke out of Aminah not removing her hijab in front of Tamika.

– She did not approve of Dee's partying and keeping bad company.

– Aminah did not like that Dee was 'friends' with young men despite knowing it is wrong in Islam.

– Aminah does not like having to come down hard on Dee all the time about her lax attitudes about religious matters, i.e., praying, fasting, mocking the religion, partying, dating, etc.

Vocabulary List:

1. Repercussions - *noun* an often indirect effect, influence, or result that is produced by an event or action
2. Assault - *noun* a threatened or attempted physical attack by someone who appears to be able to cause bodily harm if not stopped
3. Skeptical - *adj.* denying or questioning the tenets of especially a religion; marked by or given to doubt
4. Stereotype - *noun* a widely held but fixed and oversimplified image or idea of a particular type of person or thing; *verb* treat or classify according to a mental stereotype
5. Influx - *noun* the process of flowing in
6. Expel - *verb* put out or expel from a place; force to leave or move out
7. Altercation - *noun* noisy quarrel
8. Verdict - *noun* (law) the findings of a jury on issues of fact submitted to it for decision; can be used in formulating a judgment
9. Prejudice - *noun* a partiality that prevents objective consideration of an issue or situation; *verb* influence (somebody's) opinion in advance
10. Motive - *adj.* causing or able to cause motion; impelling to action
11. Bias - *noun.* Prejudice in favor of or against one thing, person, or group compared with another, usually in a way considered to be unfair
12. Judgmental - *adj.* depending on judgment
13. Controversial - *adj.* giving rise or likely to give rise to public disagreement
14. Khimar - *noun* a headscarf worn by observant Muslim women that hangs down to just above the waist
15. Wudhu - *noun* ritual ablution performed before prayer.
16. Ablution - *noun* the ritual washing of a priest's hands or of sacred vessels

Level I

1. Create a word search.
2. Define It! Match the words to the definition.
3. Create sentences with the words found from the dictionary.
4. Vocabulary: Unscramble the words.
5. Create a word map (examples here: http://www.readingrockets.org/strategies/word_maps/).
6. Guess the word: write a word on the board. Choose one student who will guess the word. The rest of the class will describe the word on the board for the student to guess.
7. Fill in the Blank

Repercussions Skeptical Influx Altercation Assault Stereotype Prejudice
Bias Expel Verdict Motive Controversial Judgmental Khimar Wudhu Ablution

1. Failing grades is one of many_____ of not attending classes.
2. Tamika was _____ as to if she would get a fair trial at her conduct hearing.
3. Stewart Hall University Apartments was known for its _____ of students due to roommate fallouts.
4. The _____ between Jennifer and Tamika left both students scarred and injured.
5. _____ and _____ were a few motives behind the Conduct Board's desire to ____ Tamika from Streamsdale University.
6. Aminah's brother is known for his _____ articles that reflect his moral views and beliefs as a Muslim.
7. Aminah performed _____ in the bathroom in preparation of prayer.
8. Dr. Sanders believed that the board was filled with _____ and that their bias and prejudice was a _____ in their guilty _____ against Tamika.
9. Tamika stopped reading Ali's editorial column because she felt he was _____ the way he spoke out against what he felt was wrong.
10. After hearing Tamika's side of the story, Dr. Sanders was convinced that the altercation between the roommates was not an _____ but rather an argument that got out of hand.
11. _____ is an important condition to perform prayer.
12. A _____ is the Islamic attire a Muslim woman wears.

Level II

1. Create a crossword puzzle with the words and their meanings
2. Create sentences with the words to ensure students understand the meaning of each word
3. Create a word map (examples here http://www.readingrockets.org/strategies/word_maps/)
4. For new words, have students try to 'guess' the meaning of the word before looking it up?
5. Guess the word: write a word on the board. Choose one student who will guess the word. The rest of the class will describe the word on the board for the student to guess.

Level I - Quiz

1. Why did Dr. Sanders want to talk to Tamika at the beginning of class?
2. How did Dr. Sanders help Tamika when the board was convinced she was a threat and ready to expel her?
3. What is the difference between bias and prejudice? Was it bias or prejudice that led to Tamika's guilty verdict? Explain your answer.
4. Why did Tamika feel like 'Dee and Muslim did not belong in the same sentence'?
5. Why was Tamika confused to learn that Aminah is 'black'?
6. Why is it dangerous to mock any part of Islam and what are the resulting consequences?

True or False (for false statements allow students to discuss the correct answer)

1. A culturally diverse conduct board would have produced a different verdict.
2. Tamika was happy to be moving out of her dorm room she shared with Jennifer and into the University Apartments.
3. Tamika was optimistic about sharing a living space with Aminah and Dee.
4. Tamika found 'ruku' the most interesting position of the Muslim prayer
5. Watching Aminah and Dee pray made her anxious and resentful of Muslims.

Level II Essay Questions

1. Explain how living with Dee and Aminah will help Tamika.
2. Explain how living with Dee and Aminah will help Tamika.
3. Explain the evidence that has Dr. Sander's convinced that bias and prejudice played a role in the board's decision. Would it have made a difference if he had called the board out on their biases and prejudices?
4. Have you ever experienced bias or prejudice? In school, work, or play? How did it make you feel? What did you do?
5. Aminah finds living with Dee stressful. Have you ever had a friend who stressed you out? How did you deal with it?

Chapter Three

1. **Discussion:** Ask students to describe the book characters introduced in Chapter 3 and use a white board to write down students' answers. *Refer to Teacher Tool Kit.

2. **Discussion:** Dr. Sanders believes that Dee and Aminah are a good combination as roommates for Tamika.

   ## Talking Points:
   – Both are nice girls.
   – They are both intelligent .
   – Islam is perfect, Muslims are not.
   – Living with them will give Tamika a chance to see Muslims at different levels of faith, Aminah being strong and Dee being weak.

> Affiliation
> Sentiment
> Insouciant
> Affable
> Implication
> Delirious
> Fundamentalist
> Contradictory
> Deduce
> Monotheism

3. **Discussion:** Explain Tamika's decision to do her research topic on Islam despite her initial bias towards Muslims.

   ## Talking Points:
   – After watching Aminah and Dee praying she was sparked with millions of questions.
   – She was curious as to what the Arabic recitation meant.
   – What made them content and spiritually connected?
   – She wanted to know what Muslims believed; she only knew they believed Jesus was a prophet, not God.
   – Her view of Muslims was based on what the media portrayed, angry black nationals, and religious fundamentalist men and oppressed women, nothing like Aminah or Dee for that matter.

4. **Discussion:** Tamika learns that Dr. Sanders is no longer a Christian. He believes in God but "takes the good of every religion." Tamika disagrees with his logic.

   ## Talking Points:
   – Tamika believed that the message in the Bible was truth and from God to her and mankind.
   – She never accepted that the divine truth was scattered in various religions.
   – Who and how does one decide what is "good" or "bad", "truth" or "falsehood" in the various religions?
   – If every person were left to sift and sort through the falsehood of different faiths to find bits and pieces of truth, each would render different results, different "truths".
   – God is not one to play games; He would never trick His creation by scattering His Divine truth and revelations in various books, mixing them with falsehood.
   – Such an ideology is contradictory to the way of God.
   – The book of God must be flawless, in one place.

TEACHER STUDY GUIDE

5. **Discussion:** Makisha is adamant in her dislike and distrust of Muslims. She tries to convince Tamika not to "let them get to her." What did she mean by that?

   ### Talking Points:
   - Cast doubt on Tamika's faith in Christianity.
   - Makisha's ex-boyfriend's sister was a Muslim.
   - Talked about the contradictions in Christianity and had Makisha doubting her religion
   - Makisha was happy to accept her mother and preacher's reasoning behind the contradictions in the religion saying, "we are not here to question God; we are just here to believe."

6. **Discussion:** In the beginning, Tamika is unsure if she should read the Qur'an. Explain her uncertainty and what led to her finally read it.

   ### Talking Points:
   - She secretly thought it would cast doubt on her faith.
   - Christians did not need it since they had the Bible.
   - She had always been warned to stay away from it by her mother and preacher.
   - Tamika reasoned she was reading it for her report not for herself so it was okay.
   - One can't fully learn and report about a faith without looking at the very foundation of the faith, its holy book.

7. **Discussion:** While reading the Qur'an, Tamika begins to feel anxiety, doubt, fear and confusion about what she believes in as a Christian and what she is reading in the Qur'an.

   ### Talking Points:
   - Muslims do believe in Jesus as a messenger of God, not his son.
   - The story of Jesus' birth is mentioned in the Qur'an, as is a similitude of his virgin birth to that of Adam who is created by God and not considered His son.
   - Tamika cannot shake the reality of the parallels in Islam and Christianity: The virgin birth, the teaching of the Gospel, and the miracles of Jesus.
   - God is enough. He does not need anyone, Jesus or otherwise.
   - In Christianity, salvation rests on belief in Jesus. In Islam, salvation rests upon belief in God alone, no father, no son.

8. **Discussion:** Internal conflict plays a big role in Tamika and Dr. Sanders' search for faith and answers. These conflicts cause each one to study Islam with different results.

   ### Talking Points:
   - Internal conflict is a mental struggle arising in a person from opposing demands or impulses.
   - Everyone at one time or another has had to deal with some kind of inner struggle.

- Tamika struggles with understanding what she believes in and finding the truth and true religion; Dr. Sanders struggled with understanding Christianity.
- Dr. Sanders turned to believing in "the good of every religion."
- Tamika continues to read the Qur'an because it questions aspects of Christianity with answers to her questions.

Vocabulary List:

1. Affiliation - *noun* the act of becoming formally connected or joined; a social or business relationship
2. Sentiment - *noun* a thought, view, or attitude, especially one based mainly on emotion instead of reason
3. Insouciant - *adj.* marked by blithe unconcern; nonchalant
4. Affable - *adj.* diffusing warmth and friendliness
5. Implication - *noun* the conclusion that can be drawn from something, although it is not explicitly stated
6. Delirious - *adj.* marked by uncontrolled excitement or emotion; experiencing delirium
7. Fundamentalist - *noun* A usually religious movement or point of view characterized by a return to fundamental principles
8. Contradictory - *adj.* unable to be both true at the same time; of words or propositions so related that both cannot be true and both cannot be false
9. Deduce - *verb* reason by deduction; establish by deduction; conclude by reasoning;
10. Monotheism - *noun* belief in a single God

Word Check: Match the words to their definitions.

Affiliation Sentiments Insouciant Affable Implication Delirious
Fundamentalists Contradictory Deduce Monotheism

1. To associate with or be connected to something or someone. _____
2. The doctrine or belief that there is only one God. _____
3. To derive a conclusion from something known or assumed. _____
4. Free from concern, worry or anxiety. _____
5. Friendly, cordial, someone who is pleasantly easy to approach. _____
6. A mental feeling, emotion, opinion or attitude toward something. _____
7. Strict adherence to the fundamental principles of any set of basic ideas, beliefs or principles. _____
8. A meaning that is not expressly stated but can be inferred and understood. _____
9. Something that is inconsistent and incompatible. _____
10. Wild with excitement. _____

Level I

1. Create a word search.
2. Define It! Match the words to the definition.
3. Create sentences with the words found from the dictionary.
4. Vocabulary: Unscramble the words
5. Create a word map - examples here   http://www.readingrockets.org/strategies/word_maps/)
6. Guess the word: Write a word on the board. Choose one student who will guess the word. The rest of the class will describe the word on the board for the student to guess.

Level II

1. Create a crossword puzzle with the words and their meanings.
2. Create sentences with the words to ensure students understand the meaning of each word.
3. Create a word map. (examples here http://www.readingrockets.org/strategies/word_maps/)
4. For new words, have students try to 'guess' the meaning of the word before looking it up.
5. Guess the word: Write a word on the board. Choose one student who will guess the word. The rest of the class will describe the word on the board for the student to guess.

Level I Quiz

1. Tamika decided to do her research paper on _____.
   - a.) Buddhism
   - b.) Islam
   - c.) Christianity

2. Tamika did not know much about Muslims except that they _____.
   - a.) Gave in charity
   - b.) Believed Jesus is a prophet not God
   - c.) Prayed five times a day

3. Dr. Sanders once considered becoming a _____.
   - a.) Buddhist
   - b.) Muslim
   - c.) Atheist

4. Makisha did not like Dee because _____
   - a.) Makisha was envious of Dee's popularity
   - b.) Makisha did not like Cubans
   - c.) Makisha did not like Muslims

5. What book did Tamika read first for her research paper on Islam? _____
   - a.) The Qur'an
   - b.) A Brief Illustrated Guide to Understanding Islam
   - c.) Fundamentals of Tawheed

True or False

1. The Holy Qur'an is the foundation of the entire faith.
2. Makisha knew Dee was a Muslim.
3. Mr. Sanders considers himself a Christian.
4. Sura Ikhas is the first sura Tamika reads.
5. Tamika's first experience reading the Qur'an scared her because it made her doubt aspects of Christianity.

Level II Essay Questions

1. Dr. Sanders can relate to Sulayman Ali and his controversial editorial articles. He says he is from the "old school" and that his parents were like him too, did not "take no stuff." What did he mean by that?
2. Summarize Dr. Sanders journey and search for faith and understanding.
3. Explain why Tamika does not agree with Dr. Sanders' belief in "some good in every religion."

4. Describe Tamika's inner conflict as she reads the Qur'an for the first time. Which verse leaves the greatest impact on her?
5. Summarize the basic similarities and differences in Islam and Christianity based on the verses Tamika read in the Qur'an.

Chapter Four

1. **Discussion:** What is Islam? Have students each give their definition of what is Islam.

   Talking Points:
   – Literal meaning: Submission or surrender
   – Application: Complete, voluntary submission to God alone

2. **Discussion:** During the interview, Tamika and Aminah discuss the fundamental differences between Islam and Christianity. Have students discuss what they are.

   Talking Points:
   – Concept of God:
   > God is the creator and everything else is creation.
   > God and creation are separate – do not overlap.
   > Creation does not share attributes of the creator.

   – The status of Jesus:
   > Jesus is a prophet.
   > Jesus is not God or the Son of God; he does not share any of God's attributes.
   > Jesus is not a savior and did not die for the sins of others.
   > Jesus was not crucified but rather raised up to the heavens.

   – Why Jesus came:
   > Jesus was a messenger of God.
   > Jesus came to bring the clear message of God to the children of Israel.

   – Who is Muhammad (pbuh)?
   > The last messenger of God.
   > He was sent to teach the true message of God.
   > He was also sent as a guide to mankind through his living examples, his Sunnah.
   > He is not a savior and cannot save anyone.

   – Muslims do NOT believe in salvation through the creation.
   – Muslims do NOT believe in crucification.

Abhorrence
Diplomatic
Savior
Innate
Rebuttal
Accountable
Covenant
Contradictory
Ostracized
Testify
Conviction
Prerequisite
Avarice
Profligate
Divinity
Khimar
Sunnah
Fitrah

3. **Discussion:** While talking, Tamika states, "None shall get to God but through him," 'through' referring to worship and 'him' referring to Jesus. Have students discuss Aminah's rebuttal to Tamika's statements.

   Talking Points:
   – The true meaning of the statement is: the only way to heaven was through following what God revealed to Jesus.
   – One cannot make up a religion and expect to go to heaven; must follow the word of God.

- The way to God is through following His prophets who came with His message; if you lived during the time of Adam, Noah, Abraham, Moses, or Jesus, you would follow the message of that prophet. Muslims follow the teachings of prophet Muhammad (pbuh) because he is the messenger of our times with the message of God.
- The message of God does not change: Worship Him and Him alone.

4. **Discussion:** On the subject of 'blind faith', Aminah tells Tamika, "You should actually know what God says, and then you believe…." Have students discuss why this is true and the possible implications of ignorance to what one follows or believes.

   ## Talking Points:
   - It is easy to be misled if you don't know what is actually said in the holy books.
   - It is easy to misinterpret a verse in the holy book if one does not understand the message.
   - One can easily spread falsehood.

5. **Discussion:** On the subject of Adab (manners), have students describe Aminah and Dee's manners and attitude during the interview toward Tamika.

   ## Talking Points:
   - They both asked questions that made Tamika think and question her understanding of Christianity.
   - They both answered her questions with a degree of confidence and knowledge of Islam, however,
   - Aminah was respectful and remained calm throughout the interview.
   - Aminah tried to make Tamika feel comfortable and relaxed to ask questions and free to express her own opinions and beliefs.
   - Aminah was patient and tolerant.
   - Dee enjoyed irritating Tamika and seeing her frustrated.
   - Dee asked Tamika thought provoking questions not to enlighten Tamika but to make her feel uncomfortable, ashamed and stupid for believing the way she did.
   - Dee criticized and ridiculed Tamika's beliefs and laughed at her.

6. **Discussion:** After the interview, Dee thinks about her actions and behavior toward Tamika. Have students describe what happened and explain why Dee's action and behavior was wrong.

   ## Talking Points:
   - It was rude; Muslims should be kind, patient, sensitive, and most of all, respectful when teaching others about Islam.
   - One of the first lessons in dawah is to never criticize another religion or belief system.
   - Her behavior could give a bad impression of Islam and Muslims.
   - Could possibly turn Tamika away from Islam.
   - Dee had no right to make Tamika feel bad about her blind faith in a religion she did not fully understand, especially when Dee herself did not follow her own faith.

7. **Discussion:** Dee reflects on her life as a Muslim beginning from her childhood up to the present. More than anyone else, she is confused by her own choices she has made throughout her life. She tries to use her memories to help her understand her path.

   ### Talking Points:
   – How her parents became Muslim when she was three and how they explained it to her (they would start to pray and they would go to heaven if they are good Muslims).
   – The meaning of her name "Durrah" (pearl) and why they gave it to her.
   – Dee thought about a slow decline in different aspects of her life: Losing her hijab, lax attitude about praying and fasting, modeling, singing and other unIslamic practices.
   – Her confusion of the many practices and beliefs in Christianity.
   – Her failure to commit to Islamic practices despite her knowing and believing the truth of Islam.
   – Her guilt and shame about her choices and failure to even try to amend her ways.
   – She doesn't even know when she started to slip in her deen.

8. **Discussion:** Tamika learns about 'Fitrah' as she reads through some of the books Aminah loans her for her research paper. Have students discuss Fitrah in Islam and how it recognizes the Oneness of Allah.

   ### Talking Points:
   – What is fitrah?
   – Everyone is born on the fitrah but is then later raised to accept the religion of their parents.

9. **Discussion:** Many people hear about Islam but do not submit. Have students discuss some of the possible factors that contribute to a person turning away from Islam after hearing about it.

   ### Talking Points:
   – Pride
   – Fear
   – Weakness
   – Holding to the religion of parents
   – Pressures from family and society

10. **Discussion:** Dee remembers a conversation with a boy in high school as they discussed who God was. She asked him to 'define God.' Have students define God.

    ### Talking Points:
    – God has attributes, certain characteristics that make him God.
    – God has absolute power.
    – God's actions are consistent with his majesty and power, his Godhood.

Vocabulary List:

Abhorrence – *noun* : a feeling of extreme disgust, aversion, abomination

Diplomatic – *adj.* skill in dealing with sensitive matters or people

Savior – *noun* a person who saves, rescues or delivers others spiritually from sin

Innate – *adj.* existing in one from birth; inborn

Rebuttal – *noun* a reply intended to show fault in an opponent's argument

Accountable – *adj.* responsible or answerable to an authority for an action

Covenant – *noun* an agreement between two or more persons to do or not to do something specified

Ostracized – *verb* to be excluded or banished from society, friendship, family, etc.

Testify – *verb* to bear witness or state something as a declaration of fact

Conviction - *noun* a fixed or firm belief

Prerequisite – *adj.* required beforehand as a prior condition

Avarice – *noun* extreme greed for riches, a desire to gain and hoard wealth

Profligate – *adj.* shamelessly immoral, wildly extravagant and wasteful

Divinity – *noun* the nature of a deity or the state of being divine

Khimar – *noun* a headscarf worn by observant Muslim women that hands down to just above the waist

Sunnah – *noun* the traditional portion of Muslim law based on the words, acts and approvals of Prophet Muhammad (pbuh)

Fitrah – *noun* the normal nature or instinct of a person animal or thing.

Level I

1. Create a word search.
2. Define It! Match the words to the definition.
3. Create sentences with the words found from the dictionary.
4. Vocabulary: Unscramble the words.
5. Create a word map - examples here: http://www.readingrockets.org/strategies/word_maps/ .
6. Guess the word: Write a word on the board. Choose one student who will guess the word. The rest of the class will describe the word on the board for the student to guess.

Level II

1. Create a crossword puzzle with the words and their meanings.
2. Create sentences with the words to ensure students understand the meaning of each word.
3. Create a word map - examples here: http://www.readingrockets.org/strategies/word_maps/.
4. For new words, have students try to 'guess' the meaning of the word before looking it up?
5. Guess the word: Write a word on the board. Choose one student who will guess the word. The rest of the class will describe the word on the board for the student to guess.

Level I Quiz

1. What is Islam and how is it different from Christianity?
2. What was the previous message of the prophets before Prophet Jesus (pbuh) and Prophet Muhammad (pbuh)?
3. How is Dee's attitude and mannerism different from Aminah's as they discuss Islam with Tamika?
4. Where does Tamika's inclination to God and spirituality originate?
5. Describe Dee's parents' reactions to her lax practices in the religion.
6. When Dee's parents' became Muslim, she was only three. How did they explain to her what "being a Muslim" was?
7. What are the proper etiquettes of giving Dawah?
8. What does Fitrah mean and why is it important?
9. What knowledge are we accountable for?
10. Why are there different religions? Give two examples in your answer.

Level II Essay Questions

1. How did Tamika's first interview go? Good or bad? Could there be room for improving Aminah and Dee's dawah practice? If so, what are they? Explain.
2. While the correct belief in God is a prerequisite for Paradise, there is more to faith, religion and going to heaven than merely "believing." Explain why this is from an Islamic perspective.
3. In trying to prove a point, Dee steps over the line and acts inappropriately. Describe what happened and how Dee's actions and behavior can cause Tamika to accept or turn away from Islam.
4. Dee found that Christians used the analogy of "an egg" to explain the trinity concept. Dee believed their analogy only proved against the concept of Trinity. Explain.
5. Retell the story of the covenant between God and Adam's offspring. Where is this story found?

Chapter Five

1. **Discussion:** Tamika did not return to her room after the interview that night. How did the discussion with Aminah and Dee make her feel? Have students discuss how Tamika may have felt.

   > Reverend
   > Logical
   > Manifest
   > Authenticity
   > Analyze
   > Pronouncement
   > Evangelical
   > Fundamental
   > Sect
   > Illiterate
   > Reference
   > Convert
   > Indicator

   ### Talking Points:
   – Tamika felt like the girls ganged up on her.

   – Tamika felt like she was being grilled as opposed to the conversation being an interview.

   – She felt suffocated by all the questions and information.

   – Aminah tried to mislead her with questions.

   – She felt slighted and angry at Dee for laughing at her.

2. **Discussion:** Makisha suggests taking drastic measures against Dee and Aminah. What does she suggest Tamika should do? Would it be productive for Tamika especially since she has to do a paper on Islam and Muslims?

   ### Talking Points:
   – She could move from the apartment.

   – File a conduct suit, calling it, "harassment" because the residential office "likes that word."

   – Tamika was not moved to take such a drastic measure because she was certain that the problem would pass and felt sure it was a misunderstanding.

   – She still needed them for her project.

   – Makisha warns that they are trying to "convert" her.

3. **Discussion:** After calming down from her conversation with Dee and Aminah, Tamika expresses her desire to know about the message of the other prophets to their people. Have students discuss the various explanations.

   ### Talking Points:
   – Makisha's response to the question is – who cares, they are dead.

   – Tamika does not accept Makisha's answer because it is in the Bible so it must be important.

   – Tamika decides to ask Makisha's uncle who is a reverend.

   – Makisha calls her uncle because she felt sorry for Tamika who was a mess and hungry for answers that will strengthen her faith.

   – When Makisha had gone through her phase of confusion, her mother was there to answer her questions and reminded her not to question God.

   – Makisha's uncle tells her, "They just told their people to do good and worship God" "….can't quite say (they worshipped Jesus) that but they worshipped God the best they could." "Jesus hadn't come yet, so uh."

- Tamika did not accept his explanation because he sounded like he was making excuses when he stuttered and took long pauses as he tried to answer her questions.
- He tries to explain that Jesus is God because they have to worship him to get to heaven, and that he is NOT God because he was also a man in flesh until he died and when the son died, God left his body.
- Tamika's mother tried to explain with an explanation that was different than Makisha's reverend uncle.
- Her mother explained the trinity as three existing all at once, and that it was God who died, not the son because only God can die for their sins, although he was the son, too.
- Tamika was upset that no one seemed to know the answer to her question or what the religion was truly founded on.

4. **Discussion:** Tamika was frustrated after talking to Makisha, her mother and Makisha's uncle. Have students describe Tamika's confusion and emotional state.

   ## Talking Points:
   - Tamika felt like her upbringing was a lie.
   - She did not know what to believe and who to trust.
   - She was even more confused with all the different explanations for Jesus' divinity.

5. **Discussion:** Summarize why Tamika has a problem with "just believing" in something she does not understand.

   ## Talking Points:
   - She did not know how to reconcile all the inconsistencies and just believe.
   - What was she supposed to believe in when everyone's explanations and interpretations were different?
   - It was difficult for her to accept a religion she did not understand, let alone try to convert people to it.
   - Was she supposed to make something up so long as it made sense to her knowing it would probably contradict another Christian's explanation?
   - Despite trying to believe, Tamika knew better and could not believe the excuses set before her by her family and friends.
   - Tamika thinks it may be her 'fitrah' that prevented her from accepting it.

6. **Discussion:** Tamika stayed with Makisha for a couple of days. Have students discuss why this actually was a good thing for Tamika and her search for the truth.

   ## Talking Points:
   - The interview sparked questions and a desire for answers.
   - Talking to Makisha and her uncle made her realize all the inconsistencies in Christianity.
   - The inconsistencies made her refuse to accept the "just believe" suggestion.
   - She became more determined to find the truth.
   - She questioned if 'Fitrah' was true.
   - Tamika continued her search for the truth even after she turned in her note cards to her professor.

7. **Discussion:** Makisha thought Tamika was being difficult, "brainwashed" by her roommates. What did Tamika do or say to make her think this way?

   ## Talking Points:
   – Tamika asked too many questions.
   – Tamika would express her frustrations.
   – Tamika kept questioning the validity of the religion.
   – Tamika would not accept her answers.

8. **Discussion:** After reading Bilal Philips, The Fundamentals of Tawheed, many of Tamika's fears were confirmed.

   ## Talking Points:
   – She was not following the religion of knowledge but the religion of her parents.
   – How can the "true religion" be confusing where everyone's concept of God was different?
   – Most Christians, if not all, were forced to rationalize and create analogies to justify their beliefs.
   – Everyone ended up with a different version of the religion.
   – Christians were commanded not to worship other gods yet the only way to heaven is by worshipping Jesus, a man.
   – How could God be just if he did not make truth clear from falsehood?

9. **Discussion:** Dee explains why she would never consider becoming a Christian. Discuss her reasons.

   ## Talking Points:
   – After reading about it, it never made sense to her.
   – It was unclear what Christians believed.
   – Some believe Jesus is God, some just that he's the Son of God and some that he's both.

10. **Discussion:** Tamika tries to explain that there are different sects in Christianity that's why there are different views. Dee explains the difference between sects in Islam and Christianity. Have students discuss the main difference.

    ## Talking Points:
    – There is only one Islam.
    – Muslims have the Qur'an and Sunnah when there is a difference of opinion among the sects.
    – Tamika is confused and asks about the 'Black Muslims'.
    – Dee explains that the "Nation of Islam" is not a sect, members are not considered Muslims because they believe that God came in the person of Fard Muhammad and that Elijah Muhammad was the messenger of God.
    – They are more of a 'reverse' Christianity than Islam.

11. **Discussion:** Dee explains that the Nation of Islam can be considered reverse Christianity. Have students analyze the difference between the two religions.

    ### Talking Points:
    – They both believe that God came down in the form of a man.
    – The NOI believe that God was a black man instead of white as portrayed in Christianity.
    – The NOI believe that white men are devils and black men are gods.

12. **Discussion:** Tamika believes that the race and color of Jesus does not matter and that is not how Christians view him. How is she wrong?

    ### Talking Points:
    – Jesus was a man, so he was of some race and of some color.
    – As a prophet, Dee explains, it is okay to view him as coming from a particular race or being of a certain color, as prophets were men from various races and cultures.
    – If he is viewed as God, then race and color matters because it can be used to further racism, supremacist views and ideologies.
    – Muslims believe that God is not a man therefore not of any race or culture.
    – No one can claim superiority because of race or color.

13. **Discussion:** Tamika learns more about Fitrah from reading Dr. Bilal Philips, The Fundamentals of Tawheed.

    ### Talking Points:
    – Everyone is responsible for belief in God on the Day of Judgment.
    – Every human being has the belief in God imprinted on his soul.
    – Throughout the course of one's life, God shows signs that the idols are not God.
    – The child follows the religion of their upbringing and custom, Allah does not hold the child accountable or punishes the child.
    – The adult however is able to distinguish truth from falsehood when clear proofs of it has been brought to him.
    – The adult must follow the religion of knowledge and reason.
    – Tamika agrees with this because it makes sense that God would have some indicator for people to know what was true from falsehood.

Vocabulary List:

Reverend – *noun* a title of respect applied to the name of a member of the clergy, church

Logical – *adj.* something that is to be expected

Manifest – *adj.* easily noticed or perceived by the eye or the understanding

Authenticity – *noun* reliable; accurate in representation of the facts

Analyze – *verb* to examine carefully and in detail so as to identify causes, key factors, possible results, etc.

Pronouncement – *noun* a formal, authoritative statement

Evangelical – *adj.* Christian churches that emphasize the teachings of the gospel

Fundamental – *adj.* serving as the foundation or essential part of something

Sect – *noun* a subdivision of a larger religious group

Illiterate – *adj.* unable to read or write

Reference – *noun* a direction in a book or writing to some other book

Convert – *noun* a person who as changed their opinion, belief, religion, etc.

Indicator – *noun* something that points to something else

Fill in the blank

1. Every Sunday, the congregation listens to the _____ give a sermon.
2. War was the _____ consequence of such threats.
3. The truth is _____ from falsehood.
4. Many people doubt the historical _____ of the Bible.
5. It takes time to thoroughly _____ something to determine its value.
6. One should be careful before making such a _____ without any proof.
7. _____ theology says that only people who have chosen to follow Jesus will get to heaven.
8. These ideas are of _____ fundamental importance.
9. There are many different _____ in Islam, but only one follows the true path.
10. His mother was ashamed to admit to her son's teacher that she was _____ and therefore could not help him with his homework.
11. The professor _____ the works of well-known scientist during his lecture.
12. Dr. Bilal Philips is a Muslim _____.
13. The lumps in the milk were a _____ that it was spoiled.

Level I

1. Create a word search.
2. Define It! Match the words to the definition.
3. Create sentences with the words found from the dictionary.
4. Vocabulary: Unscramble the words.
5. Create a word map (examples here   http://www.readingrockets.org/strategies/word_maps/).
6. Guess the word: Write a word on the board. Choose one student who will guess the word. The rest of the class will describe the word on the board for the student to guess.

Level II

1. Create a crossword puzzle with the words and their meanings.
2. Create sentences with the words to ensure students understand the meaning of each word.
3. Create a word map (examples here http://www.readingrockets.org/strategies/word_maps/).
4. For new words, have students try to 'guess' the meaning of the word before looking it up?
5. Guess the word: Write a word on the board. Choose one student who will guess the word. The rest of the class will describe the word on the board for the student to guess.

Level I Quiz

1. Why is Tamika even more confused after speaking to Makisha's uncle?
2. Why does Makisha think Tamika is 'brainwashed'?
3. Why doesn't Tamika want to press charges or move out from the apartment?
4. What did Dee mean by the Nation of Islam was like a 'reverse Christianity'?
5. Tamika struggles to accept what she was raised to believe. When she seeks answers, what does she find?

True or False

1. Tamika stayed with Makisha because she was afraid of Dee and Aminah. ____
2. Tamika's fitrah prevented her from believing what her mother and reverend said about Jesus and the message of the other prophets. _____
3. Followers of the Nation of Islam are considered Muslims. _____
4. Dee was very nervous as she apologized for her behavior. _____
5. Tamika was mad because no one could answer her questions. _____
6. We are all responsible for belief in God on the Day of Judgment. _____
7. God being of a particular race or color can further racism. _____
8. Dee wouldn't convert to Christianity because she doesn't like all the strict rules. ____
9. Dee invites Tamika to go shopping for a handbag for the formal. _____
10. Doing something fun with Tamika was a way for Dee to make amends for her poor conduct during the interview. _____

Level II Essay Questions

1. Tamika's interview caused her to question everything she believed in. Explain.
2. Compare and contrast the different explanations of Makisha's uncle and Tamika's mother.
3. Dr. T.V.N Persuade, concerning the scientific miracles found in the Qur'an, is convinced that the Quran is divine inspiration sent to Prophet Muhammad (pbuh). Explain what led him to this conclusion.
4. Describe Tamika as an adolescent.
5. After analyzing her own situation, what conclusion did Tamika come to regarding her faith? Explain your answer.
6. Tamika asks Dee if she ever considered becoming a Christian. Explain Dee's answer.

Chapter Six

1. **Location:** Dee's car on the way to Atlanta.

2. **Discussion:** The girls have quite a lot in common. Have students discuss some of their similarities.

   ### Talking Points:
   – Dee and Tamika both like to sing.
   – Both want to sing professionally.
   – Their parents are against them singing.
   – Tamika has been writing songs and poems since she was little.
   – Dee has always wanted to write songs but could never think of anything to write.

> Jocular
> Deception
> Stupor
> Ad-lib
> Ecstatic
> Exhibit
> Downplay
> Emphatic
> Fret
> Procrastinate

3. **Discussion:** When asked to sing, Tamika at first refuses. How does Dee help her get over her nervousness?

   ### Talking Points:
   – Dee promised she would not laugh.
   – Dee threatened to pull over on the side of the highway.
   – Dee sang a song first.

4. **Discussion:** Tamika sings one of her own songs for Dee. Why was this song important to her?

   ### Talking Points:
   – She made it up when she was thirteen.
   – It was her favorite song.
   – She had never sung it for anyone before, not even her family.
   – The song had great meaning to her because it represented a troubled time in her life.

5. **Discussion:** Have students read Tamika's song again. Have them analyze her song for meaning.

   ### Talking Points:
   – She does not love life anymore.
   – There is much pain in her life.
   – She has many unanswered questions that make her believe that she is not being told everything or that there is more for her to know.
   – She does not want to fear anymore.

6. **Discussion:** Summarize the back-story of how Tamika came to write this poem.

Talking Points:
– Tamika never knew her father.
– Her mother did not like to talk about him to Tamika.
– He walked out on the family when she was just a baby.
– As a child, she always wondered if he left because she was too much trouble.
– She would cry many nights because no one would help her understand.
– Not knowing about her father left an immeasurable emptiness in her life.
– She often stared at other families and wondered why she did not have a father.

7. **Discussion:** Dee seems almost guilty and sad as she tells Tamika that she wants to sing professionally. What are some reasons causing her feel this way?

Talking Points:
– Dee's parents do not want her to sing.
– Dee explains that they are Muslims.
– Dee fumbles for an explanation that is truthful but also protects her own faults.
– Muslim women are not supposed to sing in public in front of men who are not her family.
– Her family does not know she wants to sing professionally.
– Dee realizes she is wrong to sing publically but it is something she wants to do anyway.

Vocabulary List:

1. Jocular - *adj.* characterized by jokes and good humor; *adv.* with humor
2. Deception - *noun* the act of deceiving; an illusory feat; considered magical by naive observers
3. Stupor - *noun* marginal consciousness; the feeling of distress and disbelief that you have when something bad happens accidentally
4. Ad-lib - *adj.* said or done without having been planned or written in advance
5. Ecstatic - *adj.* feeling great rapture or delight
6. Exhibit - *noun* an object or statement produced before a court of law and referred to while giving evidence; something shown to the public
7. Downplay - *verb* understate the importance or quality of; represent as less significant or important
8. Emphatic - *adj.* forceful and definite in expression or action;
9. Fret - *noun* a small bar of metal across the fingerboard of a musical instrument; when the string is stopped by a finger at the metal bar it will produce a note of the desired pitch; an ornamental pattern consisting of repeated vertical and horizontal lines (often in relief)
10. Procrastinate - *verb* postpone doing what one should be doing; postpone or delay needlessly

Level I

1. Create a word search.
2. Define It! Match the words to their definition.
3. Create sentences with the words.
4. Vocabulary: Unscramble the words.
5. Create a word map (examples here http://www.readingrockets.org/strategies/word_maps/).

Level II

1. Create a crossword puzzle with the words and their meanings.
2. Create sentences with the words to ensure students understand the meaning of each word.
3. Create a word map (examples here http://www.readingrockets.org/strategies/word_maps/).
4. For new words, have students 'guess' the meaning of the word before looking it up.

Writing Exercise: Assign students to write a short Islamic fiction story. They may choose any genre for their stories. Maximum word count for the story for Level I students is 800 words. Maximum word count for Level II students is 1,200 words. Provide students with a copy of the document – *Islamic Fiction Definition and Fiction Writing Review* – found in the Teacher Tool Kit (G).

Note ⇨ The teacher may choose to provide students with the document, *A Quick Grammar Review,* found in the Teacher Tool Kit (D).

Level I Quiz

1. What little Tamika knows about her father she learned from:

   a) Her mother
   b) Her aunt
   c) Her uncle
   d) All of the above

2. Why is Tamika's mother adamant about her not singing as a career?

   a) She wanted Tamika to go to college
   b) She would only be a statistic in the music industry
   c) The music industry would snatch away her innocence,
   d) All of the above

3. What do Tamika and Dee have in common?

   a) They both want to sing professionally
   b) They both write songs
   c) They both grew up without their fathers
   d) All of the above

4. Dee hasn't told her parents about her desire to go professional because:

   a) They will not agree with it
   b) They refuse to speak to her
   c) She is not sure if she will make it pro
   d) All of the above

5. Dee asks Tamika to:

   a) Write a song for her
   b) Sing a song with her
   c) Perform at the formal with her
   d) All of the above

True or False

1. Tamika was excited to get a chance to sing for Dee, who was known for her talented vocals. _____
2. Tamika sang one of her favorite church songs. _____
3. Tamika's song is about a particular hurtful moment in her life. _____
4. Tamika grew up with a father figure. _____
5. Tamika's mother advised her never to get married. _____
6. Singing with Dee at the formal would be a foot in the door for Tamika. _____
7. Dee decided to tell Tamika her news about the producer because Aminah was at her parents for the weekend. _____

8. Tamika's aunt told her about her father because she was mad at Tamika's mother for not being open with her. _____

Level II Essay Questions

1. Do you think knowing the truth about her father, whatever it is, would have given Tamika any peace of mind growing up? Explain your answer.

2. Do you think it was right for Tamika's aunt to tell her about her father when she knew her mother did not want her to know? Explain your answer.

3. Tamika did not plan on talking about her father to Dee. Do you think it helped her being able to talk out her frustrations and pains? How? Explain your answer.

4. Why does Dee not want to tell her family she wants to sing professionally when they already know she sings in the pageants? Is it shame, regret, fear, etc.? Explain your answer.

5. Why is Tamika's mother adamant that the music industry is not right for Tamika? Is she right or wrong in her assumptions? Explain your answer.

Chapter Seven

1. **Discussion:** Tamika and Dee behave differently when they are alone and Aminah is not around.

    Talking Points:

    – They spent the weekend selecting songs from Tamika's collection.

    – They sang songs together, each picking their favorite songs.

    – They laughed and joked together.

    – When Aminah returned from home on Sunday, their fun came to a sudden halt.

    – Dee told Tamika not to tell Aminah about her performance at the formal.

    – Tamika folded the paper so Aminah could not see the songs.

2. **Discussion:** Tamika wishes she could help Dee and talk to her parents for her. What frustrates Tamika the most about Dee's situation? Why do you think she feels this way?

    Talking Points:

    – Dee has to hide what she really wants to do from her parents and Aminah; sing.

    – Tamika feels Dee's family is being selfish by imposing such strictness on Dee.

    – She wishes she could yell at them.

    – Tamika wonders why parents have to live through their children instead of living their own lives.

    – Tamika believes people should be able to live their own lives; do what they want to do.

3. **Discussion:** Tamika feels sorry for Dee yet she is in the same boat as her.

    Talking Points:

    – Tamika's mother is a strict Christian and parent.

    – She is making Tamika finish school instead of going after a singing career.

    – Tamika is also afraid to face her mother about her desires to sing professionally.

    – Tamika does not date due to her upbringing.

4. **Discussion:** Dee and Aminah both have different effects on Tamika when she is around them. How is she different around each girl?

    Talking Points:

    Dee:

    – Tamika is carefree; she does not worry about any of the important things in her life like her spirituality, her academics, etc.

    – Tamika is encouraged to pursue her own goals and dreams.

> Impose
> Strict
> Sympathy
> Evoke
> Feign
> Proximity
> Inconspicuous
> Amidst
> Resonate
> Veracity
> Haranguing
> Detrimental

IF I SHOULD SPEAK

- Tamika is attracted to Dee's worldly appeals, her beauty, her talents, and her love of shopping, carefree spirit.

Aminah:
- Tamika does not really like Aminah but she tends to make Tamika more focused.
- When Aminah is around, Tamika studies more, especially about Islam and doing research for her paper.
- Aminah appeals more to Tamika's spiritual inclination.

5. **Discussion:** After Dee leaves for a study group, Tamika finally gets around to reading the pamphlet Aminah left for her, "What Is Islam and Why You Should Be a Muslim."

Talking Points:
- One section grabs her attention because it is a question she asked Aminah during their interview: Why are there different religions.
- Due to historical factors, the three Abrahamic faiths evolved.
- There are three main religions, Judaism, Christianity, and Islam.
- Tamika knew that Paul had influenced the religion of Christianity.
- The Bible had gone through changes.
- When questioned, Tamika would say those changes were 'inspired by God'.
- Tamika began to question the validity of that claim that Paul was inspired by God to make the changes in the Bible.
- How could God 'inspire' a book that was wrong in the first place?
- Did He need humans to proofread or correct His revelation?
- Tamika begins to wonder if she is a 'disbeliever'.

6. **Discussion:** Throughout her reading, Tamika's greatest fear is if she is a disbeliever. Why?

Talking Points:
- She learns that anyone who rejects God and his messenger is a disbeliever.
- A disbeliever is one who associates partners with God.
- A disbeliever rejects the message of Allah, after they have heard it.
- Tamika has never understood the inconsistencies of Christianity, but she continued to worship a man, not God.

7. **Discussion:** For every question Tamika has or has had growing up, she finds the answers in "The Amazing Claim of Modern Day Christianity."

Talking Points:
- God's message is and always will be the same message – The path to heaven is through worshipping God alone.

- The message only changed during the time of Paul who compiled and edited the Bible of Jesus (as) after he was raised up.
- Paul introduced the concept of Trinity to the Christian Church after Jesus (as) was not on Earth.
- There is no quote from Jesus (as) in the Bible that claims the validity of the Trinity.
- Jesus (as) did not claim that his entire purpose on Earth was to be worshipped or as a savior of others' sins.
- He did not claim to be God.
- His miracles were meant to guide people – not prove his divinity.

8. **Discussion:** Finally convinced of the truth of Islam, Tamika is still not ready to face the truth. Have students discuss why she is procrastinating.

Talking Points:
- She is not ready to face the truth.
- It would mean too many changes in her life.
- She would have to acknowledge the need to give up far too many things.
- She thinks that maybe she could do it later; after having a singing career.
- She only wants to know the truth and what is next for her.

9. **Discussion:** Tamika believes that everything happens for a reason. Was it coincidence or pre-destiny that has led Tamika to where she is today? Have students recall in order all the events that has led her to her belief that Islam is the truth.

Talking Points:
- Tamika gets kicked out of her dorm.
- She moves in with two Muslims.
- She chooses Islam as her class topic for her research paper.
- She is given literature for her paper that also causes her to question the validity of her Christian beliefs.
- She finds answers to many of her unanswered questions.

10. **Discussion:** Tamika wants to convert, but many fears and obstacles are holding her back. What are they?

Talking Points:
- What would she say to her mother, Makisha?
- She is afraid her family and friends would think she had gone nuts.
- She is afraid they won't understand.
- She is not ready to give up everything.
- She still has questions regarding covering, singing, men and women relationships, marriage and more.
- She lacks the knowledge of many Islamic practices like how to pray.

Vocabulary List:

1. Impose - *verb* impose something unpleasant; impose and collect
2. Strict - *adj.* severe and unremitting in making demands; rigidly accurate; allowing no deviation from a standard
3. Sympathy - *noun* an inclination to support or be loyal to or to agree with an opinion; sharing the feelings of others (especially feelings of sorrow or anguish)
4. Evoke - *verb* call to mind; summon into action or bring into existence, often as if by magic
5. Feign - *verb* make believe with the intent to deceive; make a pretense of
6. Proximity - *noun* the property of being close together
7. Inconspicuous - *adj.* not prominent or readily noticeable
8. Amidst - in the midst or middle of; surrounded or encompassed by
9. Resonate - *verb* be received or understood; sound with resonance
10. Veracity - *noun* unwillingness to tell lies
11. Haranguing –verb lecture (someone) at length in an aggressive and critical manner.
12. Detrimental - *adj.* (sometimes followed by `to') causing harm or injury

Level I

1. Create a word search.
2. Define It. Match the words to the definition.
3. Create sentences with the words.
4. Vocabulary: Unscramble the words.
5. Create a word map - examples here http://www.readingrockets.org/strategies/word_maps/ .

Level II

1. Create a crossword puzzle with the words and their meanings.
2. Create sentences with the words to ensure students understand the meaning of each word.
3. Create a word map - examples here http://www.readingrockets.org/strategies/word_maps/ .
4. For new words, have students 'guess' the meaning of the word before looking it up?

Level I Quiz

1. Dee warns Tamika not to tell Aminah about the singing. Explain why.
2. Why is Tamika so angry with Dee's parents?
3. Why does Tamika wish Aminah did not live in the apartment with them?
4. What are the three Abrahamic faiths and how did they come to be?
5. Why is Tamika hesitant to accept Islam when she is convinced of its truth?

True or False

1. Tamika is not impressed that Dee studies very little and still gets good grades. _____
2. Dee does not want Aminah to know she is going to sing at the formal. _____
3. Dee does not like hearing about how her parents became Muslim and how Islam changed them because it reminds her of her own lack in faith. _____
4. Something in Tamika pushed her to continue reading about Islam even though she would possibly learn the truth that her faith is wrong. _____
5. Even after reading from the pamphlet, Tamika still had doubts Islam was the true religion. _____
6. Tamika's greatest fear is that she is a disbeliever. _____
7. Tamika felt weak, knowing God was watching her, waiting to see what she would do, what she would choose. _____
8. Tamika believes everything that happened to her that led up to this point was coincidence. _____
9. Tamika did not want to convert until she had the courage to tell her mother and Makisha. _____

Level II Essay Questions

1. Why do you think Dee seeks to evoke sympathy from Tamika whenever she talks about her family or weakness of faith in Islam? Explain.
2. Tamika believes everything happens for a reason. Why does she feel this way? Do you agree? Explain.
3. Finally convinced of the truth of Islam, Tamika is still not ready to face the truth. Why?
4. Indecision and procrastination is a character trait of Tamika's. Explain.
5. What are the three Abrahamic faiths? Explain the historical evolution of the three faiths?

Chapter Eight

1. **Discussion:** Have students describe Aminah's personality and conduct when dealing with Tamika.

   ### Talking Points:
   – Outspoken
   – Strong-minded
   – Tells it like it is
   – Honest and straightforward

2. **Discussion:** Tamika and Aminah discuss the causes of her doubts about Islam. What are they? Have students make a list of other common concerns many non-Muslims may have when studying Islam.

   ### Talking Points:
   – Modesty: wearing the hijab, the Abiyah or long dress and covering in general. They talk about who sets the line when it comes to what is and is not modest. Society, individuals or God?
   – Singing: It's prohibition for women in mixed company; purpose of singing; the industry in general; it's benefits and harms.
   – Aminah explains that for many of the Islamic laws including singing and sitting in mixed company, the laws serve as a protective action rather than an assumption or accusation against man.

3. **Discussion:** Tamika refers to the head covering as a "sheet". Discuss Aminah's reaction or lack of reaction. Then have students discuss how they would react to someone showing lack of respect in at least learning the proper name of the head covering.

   ### Talking Points:
   – Aminah smiled complacently.
   – She was not stirred by the comment.
   – Aminah remained calm and objective, answering the question rather than the disrespectful comment.
   – Why would Tamika refer to the Muslim head covering as a sheet instead of asking what it is called?
   – How would you react to someone calling the Islamic headdress a 'sheet'?

4. **Discussion:** Tamika has many concerns and questions. Are they out of an earnest desire to know the truth or a reason to find fault in Islam and justify not converting?

   ### Talking Points:
   – Tamika shows her displeasure of the hijab by contorting her face when she asks about it, calling it a sheet.

> Complacent
> Stipulate
> Violate
> Tempt
> Flaunt
> Indecency
> Exploit
> Adultery
> Fornication
> Accusation
> Entice
> Assumption
> Bigot
> Peremptorily
> Subjugated
> Mandates

TEACHER STUDY GUIDE

- She thinks a woman should be able to wear whatever she wants.
- She tries to find any excuse for it (covering) to be wrong.
- She argues for the sake of arguing even when she knows she is wrong. Despite being shown the truth, she still 'does not agree with it'.
- Who defines what's modest? Tamika says society and culture does. Aminah says God defines what is modest. She references the Bible and the fact that many religious women of other faiths cover modestly. Even Mary (as) is pictured covered in large flowing garments with her head covered.

5. **Discussion:** Tamika would prefer to know the truth of Islam later in life. Discuss her reasoning behind her preference.

   ### Talking Points:
   - Life is just beginning for her.
   - She wants to be able to do whatever she wants, like sing professionally, wear whatever she wants.
   - She wants to live and enjoy life; have fun first before settling down to become religious.
   - She hopes to be famous and rich first so that it won't matter if she can no longer sing professionally.

6. **Discussion:** Have students name a few misconceptions Tamika has about Muslims.

   ### Talking Points:
   - Women who cover their faces and wear niqab are a different type of Muslims.
   - She thinks married women have to cover their faces.
   - Tamika thinks the niqab is extreme.
   - She thinks polygamy is unfair.

7. **Discussion:** Tamika claims she can't accept a religion where men can oppress women. What evidence does Tamika have that makes her believe Islam allows oppression? Have students discuss Aminah's response.

   ### Talking Points:
   - She only knows what is in the media or what she's heard others say.
   - Tamika has never met a Muslim before so she does not know firsthand if they oppress women.
   - Tamika thinks that a woman is oppressed because she has to 'listen to the man'.
   - Tamika feels embarrassed once the obvious is made clear; she realizes her assumption was bigoted.
   - Oppression is not allowed in Islam even though there are some men who do oppress their wives and women in general.
   - Islam is perfect, Muslims are not.

8. **Discussion:** Tamika assumes all Muslims go out and fight innocent people in the name of God. Explain her assumptions.

Talking Points:

— Hearsay: Tamika was repeating what she heard other people say about Muslims and Jihad.

— Biased media: the media sets up stereotypes that are often misleading and false.

— Tamika refers to Jihad as 'holy war' because it is a term that the media uses to paint an unfavorable view of Muslims.

9. **Discussion:** Tensions between Dee and Aminah are rising. What is causing them and can they be improved? How?

Talking Points:

— Dee does not like Aminah nagging her all the time.

— When she returned from study Dee wanted to sleep but Aminah kept reminding her to pray.

— Dee wants Aminah to worry about herself and leave her alone.

— Aminah is adamant about reminding Dee of her prayers and does not care that she annoys Dee.

— Aminah is displeased with Dee for not praying before going to sleep. She does not like that Dee ignores her Islamic duties.

10. **Discussion:** Tamika considers being a Muslim like Dee. What does that mean and why would it be bad for her?

Talking Points:

— Like Dee, Tamika wants to be able to do whatever she wants.

— Dee does not live her life according to Islam nor does she seem to care that she is disobeying God.

— Tamika may not like or understand some things about Islam, by nature, Tamika is God-fearing and one to follow rules. She would not be able to live her double life, a life of sin after knowing the truth.

Vocabulary List:

1. Complacent - *adj.* contented to a fault with oneself or one's actions
2. Stipulate - *verb* specify as a condition or requirement in a contract or agreement; make an express demand or provision in an agreement
3. Violate - *verb* be in violation of (as of rules or patterns)
4. Tempt - *verb* try presumptuously; dispose or incline or entice to
5. Flaunt - *noun* the act of displaying something ostentatiously; *verb* display proudly
6. Indecency - *noun* an indecent or improper act; the quality of being indecent
7. Exploit - *noun* a notable achievement; *verb* use or manipulate to one's advantage
8. Adultery - *noun* extramarital sex that willfully and maliciously interferes with marriage relations
9. Fornication - *noun* voluntary sexual intercourse between persons not married to each other
10. Accusation - *noun* an assertion that someone is guilty of a fault or offence; a formal charge of wrongdoing brought against a person; the act of imputing blame or guilt

11. Entice - *verb* provoke someone to do something through (often false or exaggerated) promises or persuasion
12. Assumption - *noun* A thing that is accepted as true or as certain to happen, without proof
13. Bigot - *noun* a prejudiced person who is intolerant of any opinions differing from his own
14. Peremptorily - *adv.* in an imperative and commanding manner
15. Subjugated - *adj.* reduced to submission
16. Mandates - *noun* an official order or commission to do something

Level I

1. Create a word search.
2. Define It! Match the words to the definition.
3. Create sentences with the words found from the dictionary.
4. Vocabulary: Unscramble the words.
5. Create a word map (examples here: http://www.readingrockets.org/strategies/word_maps/).
6. Guess the word: Write a word on the board. Choose one student who will guess the word. The rest of the class will describe the word on the board for the student to guess.

Level II

1. Create a crossword puzzle with the words and their meanings.
2. Create sentences with the words to ensure students understand the meaning of each word.
3. Create a word map (examples here http://www.readingrockets.org/strategies/word_maps/).
4. For new words, have students try to 'guess' the meaning of the word before looking it up?
5. Guess the word: Write a word on the board. Choose one student who will guess the word. The rest of the class will describe the word on the board for the student to guess.

Level I Quiz

1. Tamika referred to the Muslim head covering as a _____.
   a) Head scarf
   b) Sheet
   c) Rag
   d) None of the above

2. Aminah does not respond angrily to Tamika because _____
   a) She is used to non-Muslims displeasure with the Muslim dress
   b) She did not hear Tamika
   c) Tamika is younger than her
   d) All of the above

3. Who defines what is modest?
   a) Culture
   b) Society
   c) God
   d) Individuals

4. Tamika has some doubts about Islam. What are they?
   a) Women can't wear what they want
   b) Men can oppress women
   c) Women can't sing in public
   d) All of the above

5. A person can have questions about faith so long as _____.
   a) It is to seek understanding
   b) To ascertain the truth
   c) It is not directed at the truth
   d) All of the above

6. Tamika does not want to know the truth of Islam yet. Why?
   a) She wants to wait till she is older
   b) She wants to have fun first, be a singer
   c) Her life is just beginning
   d) All of the above

7. Tamika could not bring herself to actually become a Muslim even though it sounded logical because _____.
   a) She could not bring herself to accept a religion that oppressed women
   b) She feared what her family and friends would say or how they would look at her
   c) She still had questions and concerns
   d) All of the above

8. Tamika hates herself for being so _____
   a) Confused
   b) Weak
   c) Indecisive
   d) All of the above

9. Tamika wishes she could be a Muslim like Dee because _____.
   a) She was a Muslim and still doing what she wanted.
   b) Dee was a kind and talented person.
   c) Dee was going places in her singing career.
   d) All of the above.

10. Tensions between Dee and Aminah are rising because _____.
    a) Dee does not like Aminah nagging her all the time.
    b) Aminah is displeased with Dee constantly ignoring her Islamic duties.
    c) Dee wants Aminah to worry about herself and leave her alone.
    d) All of the above.

Level II Essay Questions

1. Tamika has many misconceptions of Islam based on her limited knowledge she gets from biased sources. How can Muslims improve the way Islam and Muslims are viewed? Explain.

2. Often non-Muslims, out of ignorance or arrogance, use words that describe aspects of Islam disrespectfully. For example, Tamika refers to the Muslim headdress as a 'sheet'. What is a good way to handle a situation like this? Have you ever been in a situation like this? How did you respond to the person?

3. Are Tamika's questions out of earnest or is she trying to find fault in Islam and justify not converting? Explain your answer.

4. The sole purpose of prohibition in Islam is to close the doors to all evils. Do you agree? Provide examples that explain your answer.

5. Tensions between Dee and Aminah are rising. Explain what is causing them and what can the girls do to improve it.

Chapter Nine

1. **Discussion:** Tamika has to visit a mosque as part of her research. Why is it important to her assignment? Have students brainstorm some benefits to her visiting a mosque.

2. **Discussion:** Tamika is not sure she wants to visit the mosque this week. What are her reservations?

Talking Points:
– Dee can't go so she has to go with Aminah.
– Tamika did not want to ride with Aminah.
– She feels uncomfortable being around Aminah.
– She will have to stay at Aminah's house.
– She doesn't know Aminah or Dee's family.
– Tamika wonders what they will talk about during the long ride together or at her home.

> Exclusive
> Elite
> Sophisticated
> Abiyah
> Jibaab
> Empowerment
> Jahiliyyah
> Expiate
> Alleviate
> Predicament
> Ascertain
> Etiquette
> Epitome

3. **Discussion:** Describe Tamika and Dee's relationship now that they are working on a project together.

Talking Points:
– Tamika feels comfortable around Dee.
– They have grown closer.
– They spent a lot of time practicing their song together.
– They talked about how their life would be once they made it big, proving their family wrong.
– Dee and Tamika began to open up to each other.
– They spent their free time simply enjoying each other's company and even studying in silence together.

4. **Discussion:** Tamika's friendship with Makisha is changing. What do you think is contributing to it?

Talking Points:
– Makisha talks less to Tamika since it had become the norm for Tamika and Dee to hang out together on campus.
– When they did talk, Makisha would ask about her health and if she'd been to church lately.
– Tamika felt awkward, aware that Makisha felt obligated, now viewing Tamika as going astray.
– Makisha's conversations with Tamika were more subtle warnings about the state of her soul than friendly exchange.
– Tamika actually enjoys that her friendship with Dee annoys Makisha because it means her popularity is growing.

5. **Discussion:** Tamika does not want to be seen riding with Aminah and her brother. Why?

Talking Points:
– Tamika is embarrassed to be seen with them.
– She is afraid what people will think and say.
– Makisha would never let her hear the end of it; will think Tamika has lost her mind.
– Being seen with them will hurt her popularity and ruin her image.
– Tamika does not like Aminah's brother.

6. **Discussion:** Tamika visits the mosque with Aminah. What is Tamika's initial impression as she pulled up to the mosque?

Talking Points:
– Tamika saw women dressed like Aminah, some in face veils and men in Arab garb.
– She saw people of different ethnicities and races greeting each other eagerly, some shaking hands other hugging each other.
– She felt like she was in another country as she watched the people greet and embrace each other.
– Tamika had never seen so many Muslims gathered at one time.
– She did not know Muslim communities existed, as Islam and Muslims were irrelevant to her.
– Tamika did not feel like she belonged.
– Tamika rubs her bare arms because she feels underdressed compared to the way Muslim women dressed and covered modestly.

7. **Discussion:** Aminah offers a hijab and abiyah to wear in the mosque. How did Tamika feel about wearing it? Was it okay for Aminah to encourage Tamika to wear it?

Talking Points:
– Aminah tells Tamika that all the women in the masjid will be wearing hijab and that she will stick out if she is not wearing one.
– Tamika agrees to wear it though she really does not want to. She does not want to stick out and it will probably make her experience at the mosque more authentic and unique when she does her paper.
– Aminah offers Tamika the abiyah because she can tell Tamika is self-conscious of how she is dressed.
– How does Aminah know? Tamika rubs her bare arms as she watches the Muslims arrive and enter the mosque.
– Tamika wearing the headscarf in the mosque is a sign of respect for a place of worship where modesty is strictly encouraged.

8. **Discussion:** Tamika sits in the lobby of the mosque instead of the prayer hall. What does she observe of her surroundings? How does it make her feel?

Talking Points:
- The lobby doors are glass and the lobby has an intercom so that the sermon can be heard in the lobby.
- Tamika noticed that the Muslims sit on the floors to listen to the sermon.
- The men sat at the front while the women sat at the back.
- She noticed that the people murmured something after each pause as a man called the athan.
- She wondered what the words meant.
- She noticed various individuals praying by themselves and then sitting down with the rest of the congregation.
- The crowd of people attending the Friday prayer amazed Tamika. They sat packed, their bodies touching each other.
- She noticed that the glass door needed cleaning.

9. **Discussion:** What is the message of the Khutbah? Have students make a list of topics the Imam covers in his speech.

Talking Points:
- The problem of the Muslim community lies in their desire to be like the non-Muslims.
- Muslims make halal haraam and haraam halal.
- Muslims tend to forget their Islamic identity and duty as they try to get ahead in life.
- It is okay to be involved in community and politics as long as we adhere to Qur'an and Sunnah

Vocabulary List:

1. Exclusive - *adj.* excluding much or all; not divided or shared with others
2. Elite - *adj.* selected as the best; *noun* a group or class of persons enjoying superior intellectual or social or economic status
3. Sophisticated - *adj.* intellectually appealing; having or appealing to those having worldly knowledge and refinement and savoir-faire
4. Abiyah - *noun* long dress worn by Muslim women (usually black)
5. Jilbaab - *noun* long dress worn by Muslim women
6. Empowerment - *noun* the act of conferring legality or sanction or formal warrant
7. Jahiliyyah - *noun* Extreme ignorance and disbelief in God. Often used to describe the era that preceded the revelation of the Qur'an, and ignorance in general.
8. Expiate - *verb* make amends for
9. Exploited - *adj.* developed or used to greatest advantage (usually in a selfish or unfair way);
10. Alleviate - *verb* provide physical relief, as from pain; make easier
11. Predicament - *noun* a difficult, unpleasant, or embarrassing situation
12. Ascertain - *verb* learn or discover with certainty; make certain of something
13. Etiquette - *noun* rules governing socially acceptable behavior
14. Epitome - *noun* a standard or typical example; person or thing that is a perfect example of a particular quality or type

Level I

1. Create a word search.
2. Define It! Match the words to their definition.
3. Create sentences with the words found from the dictionary.
4. Vocabulary: Unscramble the words.
5. Create a word map (examples here   http://www.readingrockets.org/strategies/word_maps/).
6. Guess the word: Write a word on the board. Choose one student who will guess the word. The rest of the class will describe the word on the board for the student to guess.

Level II

1. Create a crossword puzzle with the words and their meanings.
2. Create sentences with the words to ensure students understand the meaning of each word.
3. Create a word map (examples here http://www.readingrockets.org/strategies/word_maps/).
4. For new words, have students try to 'guess' the meaning of the word before looking it up?
5. Guess the word: Write a word on the board. Choose one student who will guess the word. The rest of the class will describe the word on the board for the student to guess.

Level I Multiple Choice Questions

1. Tamika spent the remainder of the week working on her lyrics for the formal. How did it make her feel?
   a) Nervous
   b) Excited
   c) Refreshed
   d) All of the above

2. Tamika worked hard to make her song _____
   a) Unique
   b) Interesting
   c) Typical
   d) All of the above

3. Why was Tamika disappointed Dee could not take her to the mosque?
   a) The visit was a major part of her assignment.
   b) Dee canceled on her at the last minute.
   c) Tamika did not know how to get to the mosque.
   d) All of the above

4. Tamika does not want to ride with Aminah and her brother because _____.
   a) Tamika does not like them.
   b) She is afraid what Makisha will think and say.
   c) She is afraid her popularity and image will suffer.
   d) All of the above

5. Tamika feels like she does not belong as part of the college society. Why?
   a) She is failing her classes.
   b) She feels discriminated against at school.
   c) She is only there because her mother wants her to be.
   d) All of the above

6. The first thing Tamika notices when she pulls up to the mosque is:
   a) The parking lot is crowded.
   b) There are people of different races and ethnicities.
   c) Women are dressed liked Aminah.
   d) All of the above

7. Aminah offers Tamika to wear _____.
   a) A jilbaab
   b) An abiyah
   c) A scarf
   d) All of the above

8. Aminah does not like it when people call the abiyah a jilbaab because_____.
   a) It can be confusing for people who are not familiar with the terms.
   b) Because it poses the danger of people misunderstanding the Qur'an since jilbaab is mentioned in the Qur'an.
   c) She is against people following their 'custom' instead of the Qur'an.
   d) All of the above

9. How did Tamika feel after the sermon?
   a) Tamika was mesmerized by the unity of the Muslim women, she felt like she belonged in the prayer hall with the praying women.
   b) Tamika was frustrated with the Imam and his sermon.
   c) The sermon only increased her doubt about Islam and certain rules.
   d) All of the above

10. Tamika felt uncomfortable around Aminah's mother. Why was it difficult to relax and greet her casually?
    a) Tamika felt intimidated by Aminah's mother.
    b) Tamika did not know where to look as she is accustomed to looking a person in the face and the veil posed a barrier between them.
    c) Tamika abhorred women who wore the face veil because it symbolized oppression by men in the religion.
    d) All of the above

Level II Essay Questions

1. Do you agree with the message of the Imam about the state of the Muslim communities? Explain your answer.
2. Do you think Tamika would have had a different experience at the mosque had she not worn the hijab and abiyah? Explain.
3. Why did Tamika have to visit a mosque as part of her assignment? Did Tamika's visit to the mosque prove useful toward her research paper about Muslims and Islam? Explain.
4. What did Tamika take away personally from her visit to the mosque? Summarize the dangers of misunderstanding the Qur'an.
5. Why does Tamika constantly feel like she is out of place and does not belong in her surroundings? Explain

Chapter Ten

1. **Discussion:** Ask students to describe Aminah and Dee's mothers (introduced in Chapter Ten). Use a white board to write down students' answers.

2. **Discussion:** How did Tamika's view and opinion of Muslims change at Aminah's house?

   > Contemplative
   > Introvert
   > Assimilation
   > Baseless
   > Volition
   > Hypocrite
   > Emphatically
   > Tahajjud
   > Kuffar
   > Inquisitive

   ## Talking Points:
   – The women looked like regular, ordinary women.
   – Sarah is white with blonde hair and freckles.
   – Underneath covering garments, Muslim women wear ordinary clothes.
   – Sarah and Dee's mother had a voice and personality.
   – They were opinionated and strong women.
   – They loved who they were and what they chose.
   – No one forced them to convert. Dee's mother actually fought the truth based on all the stereotypes and things she heard about Islam before accepting it.
   – No one asked or told them they had to cover, they did it because God wanted them, too.
   – Tamika was surprised by the striking contrast between how she viewed Muslim women and Islam and the reality she witnessed.

3. **Discussion:** Did Dee's family react appropriately to Naimah's line of questioning Tamika and claiming she was going to hell for not being a Muslim?

   ## Talking Points:
   – Aesha remarks that Tamika is not Muslim.
   – She tells Naimah she shouldn't say Tamika is going to the hell fire.
   – Her mother reminds her that not everyone is a Muslim.
   – Her mother picks her up and takes her out of the room.
   – Her mother apologizes for Naimah's comments.

4. **Discussion:** Four-year-old Naimah believes Tamika is going to go to hell because she does not pray and is not a Muslim. How does that make Tamika feel?

   ## Talking Points:
   – Tamika felt dirty, as if she were a heathen.
   – She knew the family did not intend to make her feel that way.
   – She thinks that the little girl vocalized what everyone else thought, but knew was impolite to say.
   – She never imagined that there were others who felt as strongly about their religion as she had of her own.

– She felt regretful of her past assumptions and ignorance about Islam and Muslims, and other faiths as well.

5. **Discussion:** After speaking and spending time with Aminah and Dee's family, Tamika realizes her ignorance toward Islam and Muslims.

   ## Talking Points:
   – She still harbored childish stereotypes about people who were unlike her.

   – Her ideas and views of Muslims and Islam were baseless.

   – Hadn't it hurt her, the mistreatment and assumptions by others based upon the color of her skin?

   – She painfully understood what it meant to be racist.

   – Was she like Jennifer, who flung a racist slur at her?

   – She held views about Islam and Muslims the same way Jennifer held views about her.

   – Like most racists, Tamika was raised upon ignorance, knowing nothing about others yet accepting as fact what the media portrayed without verifying it for herself.

   – Was she a hypocrite? Claiming to be a victim of racism and prejudice while at the same time holding prejudiced and biased views about others who were different?

6. **Discussion:** Aminah vents her frustrations to her mother about her relationship with Durrah.

   ## Talking Points:
   – Aminah tries to remind Dee of her duties but Dee only listens sometimes.

   – Dee has been resistant and irritable lately.

   – Dee does not talk to Aminah anymore, does not confide in her, share her worries.

   – Aminah is tired and does not want to think about Dee's lack of religious commitment.

   – She complains that Durrah is not the same person or same friend anymore.

   – She is tired of babysitting Durrah.

   – Their living arrangements were taking a toll on her faith and ability to practice Islam.

7. **Discussion:** Sarah listens to her daughter vent her frustrations and understands how association leads to assimilation. Have students discuss what it means and why Sarah is worried about Aminah.

   ## Talking Points:
   – Peer pressure is highest amongst friends and peers.

   – College life is fast paced.

   – The social arena is very alluring with the partying, drugs, music, etc.

   – The pressure to "fit in" with the crowd (image, social status, etc.).

   – No one is immune to temptation, not even Aminah.

   – One is more likely to try something out if their friend suggests it.

8. **Discussion:** Aminah wants to do Da'wah to Tamika. What does she find to be her biggest obstacle? Why?

   ### Talking Points:
   – She can't get close to Tamika when Dee is around.
   – Dee is a distraction to Tamika.
   – Dee and Tamika have more in common.
   – Dee gives the wrong example of how a Muslim woman should behave in public.

9. **Discussion:** Tamika is quite impressed with Kevin. Have students make a list of the things she finds admirable about him.

   ### Talking Points:
   – His appearance: he is tall and handsome, she is not sure of his ethnicity – Hispanic, American, possibly some Asian.
   – His house: quiet, soft music in the background, fresh and pleasant smell.
   – His studio: the basement was carpeted, neatly arranged with tape and CD shelves along the wall, and appeared professional.
   – Recording equipment lined one wall while an enclosed glass room contained microphones.
   – Kevin was fully equipped for the job as a recorder.

10. **Discussion:** After leaving Kevin's that night, Tamika's mind was filled with curiosity and suspicions. Summarize the events that led up to her feeling this way.

    ### Talking Points:
    – Dee was dressed up and wearing perfume.
    – The playful exchange between Kevin and Dee.
    – They stayed late chit-chatting.
    – Tamika felt uneasy, as if she were intruding in a private moment between the two.
    – Kevin's refined manners.
    – Kevin asked Dee to give him a call.
    – Dee's expression in the car after leaving Kevin's and during the drive back to the apartment.

Vocabulary List:

1. Contemplative - *adj.* expressing or involving prolonged thought
2. Introvert - *noun* a person who tends to shrink from social contacts and to become preoccupied with their own thoughts
3. Assimilation – noun the act of people of different backgrounds coming to see themselves as part of a larger national family
4. Baseless - *adj.* without a basis in reason or fact
5. Volition - *noun* the act of making a choice; the capability of conscious choice and decision and intention
6. Hypocrite - *noun* a person who professes beliefs and opinions that he or she does not hold in order to conceal his or her real feelings or motives
7. Emphatically - *adv.* without question and beyond doubt
8. Tahajjud. - noun very late night prayer.
9. Kuffar - noun those who deny or disbelieve in God
10. Inquisitive - *adj.* showing curiosity; inquiring or appearing to inquire

Level I

1. Create a word search.
2. Define It! Match the words to their definition.
3. Create sentences with the words found from the dictionary.
4. Vocabulary: Unscramble the words.
5. Create a word map (examples here   http://www.readingrockets.org/strategies/word_maps/).
6. Guess the word: Write a word on the board. Choose one student who will guess the word. The rest of the class will describe the word on the board for the student to guess.

Level II

1. Create a crossword puzzle with the words and their meanings.
2. Create sentences with the words to ensure students understand the meaning of each word.
3. Create a word map (examples here http://www.readingrockets.org/strategies/word_maps/).
4. For new words, have students try to 'guess' the meaning of the word before looking it up?
5. Guess the word: Write a word on the board. Choose one student who will guess the word. The rest of the class will describe the word on the board for the student to guess.

Writing exercise: Awkward Moments – Assign the students to write a 500-800 word essay describing an awkward moment in their life.

**Note ⇨ The teacher may choose to provide students with the document, *A Quick Grammar Review* found in the Teacher Tool Kit (D).

Level I Quiz

1. What did Tamika learn by talking to Aminah and Sarah?
2. How did Tamika feel when Naimah said she was going to go to Hell for not being a Muslim?
3. When did Tamika realize her views about Muslims could be considered "racist"?
4. How does association lead to assimilation?
5. Aminah did not want to share what she felt about Durrah. Why?
6. Why did she finally tell her mother what was on her chest?
7. Why is Aminah worried about Durrah?
8. How is Naimah similar to Durrah when she was a small child?
9. Why doesn't Aminah want to live with Durrah anymore?

Level II Essay Questions

1. What is the irony of Dee's sister, Naimah, saying Tamika is going to go to hell for not being a Muslim? Explain
2. Sarah explains that it is common for many Muslims born into Muslim families go through changes before coming back to Islam. Do you agree with this statement? Explain your answer.
3. "Each person is on the path of his or her friend." What does this mean? Do you feel it is mostly true for you? Explain your answer.
4. Sarah tells Aminah "the most important thing for her to focus on is being an example" in her relationship with Dee? Do you agree? Explain your answer.
5. Have you ever had a friend you thought was going astray (decline in faith, hanging out with bad company, getting into trouble, etc.)? What did you do? Were you able to help your friend? How?

Chapter Eleven

1. **Discussion:** Tamika overhears Dee talking on the phone and is concerned for her. She has her suspicions but is not really sure. Ask students to contemplate what is causing Tamika's concern for Dee.

Talking Points:
— Dee constantly talks about her singing career and how her parents wouldn't approve.
— The night before she noticed how happy Dee was with Kevin.
— Dee is being pressured to talk to her parents by the caller, Kevin maybe?
— Dee is really afraid to face her parents with her life goals.

2. **Discussion:** Ask students to describe Tamika's reaction to seeing Dee crying. What reason did she have to feel so ashamed?

Talking Points:
— Tamika felt like she was invading Dee's private moment.
— Tamika felt like she had eavesdropped on part of Dee's conversation.
— Tamika was curious but did not feel like it was right to ask about what was going on.
— She was embarrassed for Dee who is usually happy and free-spirited.

3. **Discussion:** Have students discuss possible outcomes HAD Tamika tried to comfort Dee and understand what was bothering her that night. Would it have made a difference for Tamika or Dee?

Talking Points:
— Dee may have opened up to Tamika had she shown concern.
— Sometimes, just talking out our frustrations allows us to reflect and come up with solutions to our problems.
— Dee may have thought Tamika was 'prying' into her business.
— Is it 'prying' when you try to get to the root of someone's problems?
— When is it not helpful to try and comfort a person or friend in distress?
— How would you (students) approach a friend or acquaintance if they were distressed or crying?

4. **Discussion:** Dee is a subject of great curiosity to Tamika. Ask students to describe Dee from Tamika's perspective.

Talking Points:
— Tamika was not sure just how Muslim Dee was. Muslim was more a family name than a belief system.

Delusion
Disheveled
Incite
Pry
Vulnerable
Inadvertently
Tranquility
Nonchalance
Tousled
Fragile
Ecstatic
Promiscuity
Vague
Vivid
Succumb
Deduce

- Tamika admired Dee's strength and will to go after her dreams.
- Dee was easy going, loved to laugh and was kind.
- Dee never had a negative word about others, always brushed their faults aside even if they outwardly scorned her. For example: she did not allow Tamika to speak negatively about Aminah and her nagging ways regarding Dee not praying, saying, "she was trying to help her (Dee) the best way she knew how."

5. **Discussion:** Ask students to explain why Durrah, Dee's Muslim name, is only used when the author follows Aminah's story line.

   ## Talking Points:
   – Aminah grew up calling her Durrah.
   – Calling her 'Dee' would force Aminah to accept Durrah's unIslamic behavior.
   – Aminah's desire to hold onto the memory of her friend when she was a strong Muslim.
   – A way to help remind 'Dee' of her Muslim identity.
   – The author's way of showing the change in Dee/Durrah's lifestyle.

6. **Discussion:** Aminah is strict praying the voluntary prayer, Duha. Have students discuss the reasons why she chooses to pray Duha.

   ## Talking Points:
   – Duha is a prayer that is prayed just after sunrise.
   – It has a minimum of two rakats and maximum of 12.
   – The Prophet said: "Whoever regularly prays the two rak`ats of Duha, his sins are forgiven even if they are as numerous as the foam of the sea." Narrated from Abu Huraira by al-Tirmidhi, Ibn Majahm and Ahmad.   http://www.livingislam.org/n/sldh_e.html#4
   – She prays duha due to its immense spiritual benefits.
   – It is a habit she is accustomed to doing since she was in high school, therefore very natural.
   – She fears abandoning the prayer will cause her to slip in her faith the same way Durrah had.
   – Durrah's change terrified her.

7. **Discussion:** Aminah does not understand the drastic and almost sudden change in Durrah's behavior and faith. She went from being strong and outspoken in her faith, to uncovering and partaking in other forms of unIslamic behavior. She reflects:

   ## Talking Points:
   – Durrah was not afraid to strike up a conversation about Islam with classmates or teachers.
   – Aminah remembers a time in high school when Durrah was asked to show her hair.
   – Aminah was shocked that Durrah showed the girls her hair.
   – Aminah wonders if all the accolade and attention about her physical beauty, for which she was not accustomed to, made Durrah want more.

- Durrah came from a loving family that showered her with compliments about her Islam but also about her physical beauty she was blessed with.
- Durrah succumbed to the whispers of evil.
- What stopped Aminah from coming to Durrah's aid when the other girls were pressuring her to show her hair?
- If Aminah had said something, would Durrah have shown her hair?

8. **Discussion:** Some may argue that Aminah's feelings toward her friend, Durrah, are self-righteousness and always looking down on her. Have students break into two groups. Group A will argue that Aminah is being self-righteous. Group B will argue that Aminah is being a good friend and looking out for Durrah's best interest by reminding her about her Islamic duties. Each group must provide proof for their arguments.

9. **Discussion:** Dee invites Tamika to go camping with her and a few friends during spring break. What are Tamika's concerns about going?

Talking Points:
- She can't afford it.
- She does not want Dee to pay for it.
- She does not know who is going, besides Dee.
- She is worried that the others will look at her funny because they don't know her.

Vocabulary List:

1. Delusion - *noun* deception by creating illusory ideas; a mistaken or unfounded opinion or idea
2. Disheveled - *adj.* in disarray; extremely disorderly
3. Incite - *verb* provoke or stir up; urge on; cause to act
4. Pry - *noun* a heavy iron lever with one end forged into a wedge; *verb* be nosey
5. Vulnerable - *adj.* capable of being wounded or hurt
6. Inadvertently - *adv.* without knowledge or intention
7. Tranquility - *noun* a state of peace and quiet
8. Nonchalance - *noun* the trait of remaining calm and seeming not to care; a casual lack of concern
9. Tousled - *adj.* untidy
10. Fragile - *adj.* vulnerably delicate; easily broken or damaged or destroyed
11. Ecstatic - *adj.* feeling great rapture or delight
12. Promiscuity - *noun* indulging in casual and indiscriminate sexual relations
13. Vague - *adj.* not clearly understood or expressed
14. Vivid - *adj.* producing powerful feelings or strong, clear images in the mind
15. Succumb - *verb* to submit to an overpowering force or yield to an overwhelming desire
16. Deduce - *verb* conclude by reasoning

Level I

1. Create a word search.
2. Define It! Match the word to the definition.
3. Create sentences with the words found from the dictionary.
4. Vocabulary: Unscramble the words.
5. Create a word map - examples here: http://www.readingrockets.org/strategies/word_maps/.
6. Guess the word: Write a word on the board. Choose one student who will guess the word. The rest of the class will describe the word on the board for the student to guess.

Level II

1. Create a crossword puzzle with the words and their meanings.
2. Create sentences with the words to ensure students understand the meaning of each word.
3. Create a word map (examples here http://www.readingrockets.org/strategies/word_maps/).
4. For new words, have students try to 'guess' the meaning of the word before looking it up?
5. Guess the word: Write a word on the board. Choose one student who will guess the word. The rest of the class will describe the word on the board for the student to guess.

Level I Quiz

1. How does Tamika respond to seeing Dee cry?
2. Why do you think Tamika responded the way she did?
3. How does Dee respond to Tamika seeing her cry?
4. What quality does Tamika like most about Dee?
5. Why does Aminah like to pray the Duhaa prayer?
6. How were Durrah and Aminah similar and different in high school?
7. What terrifies Aminah most as she contemplates Durrah's change?
8. What does Aminah think psychologists would deduce from Durrah's transformation from highly religious to barely practicing?
9. What would you say Tamika and Dee get out of their friendship?
10. Where does Dee invite Tamika to spend Spring break?

Level II Essay Questions

1. Dee is conflicted by her desire to have a successful career and her desire to smooth things over with her family. How is it affecting her?
2. Dee has no problems with singing, modeling and uncovering. It is a lifestyle and choice she is comfortable with. Why do you think she has a hard time facing her parents with the truth about her desire to go professional knowing she already has their disapproval of her current lifestyle?
3. Do you agree with Aminah's assumption that Durrah's lifestyle is a 'need for attention', attention she did not get from home? Explain your answer.
4. What emotions do you think is going through Aminah as she reflects about the changes in her friend, Durrah? Ex: anger, fear, regret, concern, etc. Explain your answer.
5. How would you describe Tamika and Dee's relationship now? Is there friendship a good thing? Will it help either girl gain a better appreciation of her faith? Why? Explain your answer.

Chapter Twelve

1. **Discussion:** How did the camping trip help Tamika?

   Talking Points:
   – Camp was relaxing.
   – The scenery gave Tamika tranquility.
   – It gave her an escape from the realities of her life and troubles like school, her spiritual struggles, her family issues.

2. **Discussion:** Dee tells Tamika that Kevin asked to marry her. While she is happy at the thought of marrying him, she is also concerned. What are her concerns?

   Talking Points:
   – She has not spoken to her family.
   – Father will not approve.
   – Parental permission is a 'rule in Islam'.
   – Kevin has not practiced Islam since he was a very young boy.

3. **Discussion:** Dee says 'yes' to Kevin's proposal despite knowing her parents will not approve. Dee tries to explain her reason to Tamika despite her own uncertainties.

   Talking Points:
   – Dee does not think Islamic rulings matter to her anymore since she does not follow them anyway.
   – She doesn't see herself as a Muslim sometimes.
   – She is considering if she wants to remain a Muslim.
   – She is tired of all the rules imposed in Islam.
   – She is worried she can't be married to Kevin if she's Muslim and he is not.
   – Kevin is practically like her, Muslim only by lineage, not by practice.

4. **Discussion:** Dee is considering whether she wants to stay a Muslim. Why does she feel this way? Will leaving Islam make her life and choices easier?

   Talking Points:
   – She is tired of all the strict rules.
   – She does not feel like she is a Muslim anymore.
   – Being a Muslim will keep her from Kevin.
   – Dee is not doing anything different now than if she were not a Muslim.
   – Removing the regret she has for doing the things she knows are wrong.

> Trepidation
> Ludicrous
> Wane
> Premature
> Sanity
> Fictitious
> Tranquility
> Ominous
> Captivate
> Attribute
> Render

TEACHER STUDY GUIDE

5. **Discussion:** Tamika is greatly affected by her conversation with Dee regarding whether Dee wants to remain a Muslim due to its strict rules. Have students discuss some of the implications of 'waiting' and 'taking her time' before becoming a Muslim from Tamika's point of view.

Talking Points:

– Gives Tamika a chance to study Islam first.

– Gives Tamika a chance to 'live' her life before becoming 'religious'.

– Tamika won't rush into something she is not ready for.

– When she does become Muslim it will be completely, not half-heartedly.

– However, procrastination may cause her to have more doubt.

– She may choose not to become Muslim due to pressures from family, career and/or society.

Vocabulary List:

1. Trepidation - *noun* a feeling of alarm or dread
2. Ludicrous - *adj.* broadly or extravagantly humorous; ridiculous
3. Wane - *noun* a gradual decline (in size or strength or power or number)
4. Premature - *adj.* uncommonly early or before the expected time
5. Sanity - *noun* normal or sound powers of mind
6. Fictitious - *adj.* formed or conceived by the imagination; not real or true, being imaginary or having been fabricated
7. Ominous - *adj.* threatening or foreshadowing evil or tragic developments
8. Captivate - *verb* attract and hold the interest and attention of
9. Attribute - *noun* a quality or feature regarded as a characteristic or inherent part of someone or something
10. Render - *verb* cause to become

Level I

1. Create a word search.
2. Define It! Match the word to the definition.
3. Create sentences with the words found from the dictionary.
4. Vocabulary: Unscramble the words.
5. Create a word map (examples here   http://www.readingrockets.org/strategies/word_maps/).
6. Guess the word: Write a word on the board. Choose one student who will guess the word. The rest of the class will describe the word on the board for the student to guess.

Level II

1. Create a crossword puzzle with the words and their meanings.
2. Create sentences with the words to ensure students understand the meaning of each word.
3. Create a word map (examples here: http://www.readingrockets.org/strategies/word_maps/).
4. For new words, have students try to 'guess' the meaning of the word before looking it up?
5. Guess the word: Write a word on the board. Choose one student who will guess the word. The rest of the class will describe the word on the board for the student to guess.

Level I Quiz

1. What did Tamika find most memorable about her Spring Break experience?
2. Why did Tamika feel paranoid toward the end of the camping trip?
3. Why is Dee afraid to tell her family about Kevin?
4. What advice does Tamika give to Dee regarding talking to her parents?
5. Where is Kevin from and how is he similar to Dee?

True or False

1. Tamika was not able to relax and concentrate for weeks after Spring break, all she could think about was becoming Muslim. _____
2. Dee does not care that Kevin is not a Muslim, she still wants to marry him. _____
3. Tamika wants to be sure and ready when she becomes Muslim. _____
4. Dee and Kevin plan to raise their children Muslim. _____
5. Things were looking up academically for Tamika. _____

Level II Essay Questions

1. Summarize Dee's concern of telling her parents about Kevin and her career goals.
2. How would marrying Kevin be a good thing for Dee? How would it be a bad thing for Dee? Explain your answers.
3. What suggestions would you give Dee regarding talking to her parents? Explain your suggestions and how they would help Dee.
4. How is Kevin 'like' Dee? Explain their similarities and differences? How do their similarities or differences influence their relationship?
5. Summarize Tamika's reasons for not becoming a Muslim right away even though she believes and knows it is the right thing to do? What does she hope to accomplish before converting?

Chapter Thirteen

1. **Discussion:** Tamika is having doubts about the Spring Formal performance that she feels will launch her into fame and fortune. What are her fears and why is this performance so important to her, beside the riches and fame?

   Talking Points:
   – Tamika was scared and nervous; it did not help that Dee was nervous as well who – Tamika' strength and support.
   – Tamika has doubts that the producer will show up, causing her to wonder why a producer would want to hear her sing.
   – Thinks that all her hopes and rehearsals have been in vain.
   – This is important to her because she wants to prove her mother wrong.
   – More importantly, prove to herself she can be the singer she has always dreamed she could be.

2. **Discussion:** Dee hoped that Aminah would be gone while she and Tamika got ready for the formal. Why would Dee care since Aminah already knew she was going to perform?

   Talking Points:
   – Dee does not want Aminah to ruin her fun.
   – Knowing Aminah disapproves will cause her to stress out.
   – Tonight is crucial for her and she needs to focus.

3. **Discussion:** Dee is known for not liking confrontation and being a 'laid back' kind of person. How does she deal with stress and the disapprovals of Aminah and her family? After using the talking points, allow students to discuss ways they avoid confrontation.

   Talking Points:
   – Dee likes to joke around to lighten the tension in a situation or conversation.
   – Dee avoids confrontation and arguing with politeness.

4. **Discussion:** Why do you think Dee is this way? Why doesn't she stand up for herself when she feels slighted by Aminah's constant reminders?

   Talking Points:
   – It is possible that while she wants to do as she pleases, a part of her still longs for the old her, the Durrah of her past, the practicing Muslim.
   – Dee has a lot of respect for her friend, Aminah
   – Dee understands that Aminah is doing her duty as a friend and a Muslim by reminding her about her Islamic duties.

Crucial
Ayatul Kursi
Kursi
Ablution
Conceal
Empathize
Sashay
Irk
Confrontation
Trivial
Diverge
Tenacious
Crescendo
Surreal

5. **Discussion:** Aminah somehow feels responsible for Dee's spiritual self. Why do you think she feels this way especially when Dee does not respond to Aminah's warnings and reminders? How does it make Aminah feel to have her reminders and warnings pushed aside as if they were jokes?

   ## Talking Points:
   – They've known each other for a long time.
   – Aminah knew Dee/Durrah when she was a strong Muslim and longs for her to return to her deen.
   – It is a duty of every Muslim to enjoin what is good and forbid what is evil.
   – Aminah feels pressured by their parents to keep Dee in check or at least bring her back to Islam.

6. **Discussion:** Tamika is still new to understanding much of the Islamic rulings of modesty to which Dee has little care for. So it infuriates her when Aminah constantly "interferes" in Dee's life. Have students explain Tamika's frustrations.

   ## Talking Points:
   – Tamika can relate to Dee in that she also wants to be a singer against her mother's warnings.
   – She doesn't like that Aminah acts like Dee's mother or overseer.
   – She feels Dee has the right to make her own decisions.
   – Her own hidden resentment she has toward her own mother for not approving of her desire to be a professional singer.

7. **Discussion:** Tamika and Dee have become very close friends. Have students discuss how this makes Aminah feel, especially since she and Dee used to be such good friends.

   ## Talking Points:
   – Envy – that Dee found someone else, less stress-provoking, not pestering, not Muslim. Dee was having fun and spending more time with Tamika. She was jealous of Dee and Tamika's friendship.
   – Hurt – that Dee no longer wanted to be around her, did not want her as a friend, moved on and found friendship with someone else; they had been through a lot.
   – Sorrow – she missed their friendship; grew up together; has to let go.

8. **Discussion:** Aminah stops herself from discussing the inappropriateness of the spring formal or reminding Durrah to say her prayers. Ask students to explain why Aminah suddenly feels the need to step back and let Durrah do her own thing.

   ## Talking Points:
   – Aminah was tired and drained from all the constant rejection of her reminders.
   – She knew Dee would not want to undo all of her makeup, hairdo or nail polish.
   – She did not want to 'pester' Dee as that was driving her away.
   – Aminah had her own soul to worry about.

9. **Discussion:** The song Dee and Tamika sing at the formal talks a lot about learning and lessons. Have students take turns reading each line then discuss the possible interpretations of the song from each girl's point of view.

   ### Talking Points:
   – How I stood, how I fell: Dee went from practicing to not practicing; Tamika went from blindly following Christianity to contemplating Islam and becoming a Muslim.

   – What of that learning, what of it today: Dee and Tamika have both 'abandoned' their childhood lessons for a chance to "make it big" as singers.

   – Is the knowledge to be lived upon, or just spoken from my tongue: Dee is only Muslim by name, not following the tenants of her faith; Tamika is Christian but practices with little understanding of her faith.

   – Dee understands her faith but does not act upon it, Tamika acts upon her faith but does not understand it.

   – With whom will I win, with whom will I lose: As Dee contemplates leaving Islam, she risks losing her family and friends while gaining a career and relationship with Kevin; As Tamika contemplates leaving Christianity, she risks losing her family, friends and dreams of singing while gaining spiritual understanding, peace of mind and stability.

   – I hear the footsteps of my thoughts: For both girls, the footsteps may represent their past and what lessons they can take from them. For Dee, remembering her past may remind her of all that she lost and rebuild her faith.

   – I try to listen, Lord knows I do: Dee often reflects on her life changes. She sometimes regrets her decisions. Sometimes she accepts Aminah's reminders by praying with her. Tamika asks questions to try to better understand her faith and to seek out the truth from the falsehood and confusion.

   – But what to make of it, for the lessons are not few: Both girls are getting tired and more confused from the constant pull of faith and family with the constant pull of their career goals and desires.

   – For I hear the voices…echoing in my head: The echoes may represent their family and friends who are trying to call them back to faith. Aminah for Dee and Makisha for Tamika.

   – But they echo…..and I feel all alone: Perhaps each girl has chosen her path that conflicts with those of her echoes, no longer heeding the reminders and warnings of family and friends. Dee giving up being a Muslim and Tamika giving up being a Christian.

10. **Discussion:** During a moment of reflection, Aminah has a moment of clarity, a moment of truth in how to win back her friend Durrah and to help guide her back to Islam. Have students summarize Aminah's plan to mend her friendship with Durrah.

    ### Talking Points:
    – She would be more subtle in her reminders so that Durrah would again appreciate Islam and Aminah.
    – She would not compromise her religion by her desire to vent.
    – She would not pester Durrah any more as it pushed her further away from Islam.
    – Aminah would go shopping with Durrah.
    – Listen to Durrah's music that does not have instruments.

- Encourage Durrah to sing for Muslim women.
- Offer constructive suggestions rather that critical.
- Laugh more with Durrah, be a friend to Durrah.
- Accept Durrah—Dee for who she is now and go from there and act as an example.
- Spend more time complementing instead of scolding Durrah, letting her know Aminah still cared and remembered their friendship and all the good times.

Vocabulary List:

1. Crucial - *adj.* of extreme importance
2. Ayatul Kursi. – The Throne Verse - a particular ayat (verse) in the Qur'an
3. Kursi – noun an Arabic word for chair or throne
4. Ablution - *noun* ritual washing
5. Conceal - *verb* prevent from being seen or discovered
6. Empathize - *verb* be understanding of
7. Sashay - *noun* walk in an ostentatious yet casual manner, typically with exaggerated movements of the hips and shoulders
8. Irk - *verb* irritate or vex
9. Confrontation - *noun*   the act of hostile groups opposing each other
10. Trivial - *adj.* obvious and dull
11. Diverge - *verb* move or draw apart; extend in a different direction
12. Tenacious - *adj.* not easily discouraged
13. Crescendo - *adj.* gradually increasing in volume
14. Surreal - *adj.* resembling a dream, bizarre

Level I

1. Create a word search.
2. Define It! Have students look up the words in a dictionary.
3. Create sentences with the words found from the dictionary.
4. Vocabulary: Unscramble the words.
5. Create a word map - examples here http://www.readingrockets.org/strategies/word_maps/.
6. Guess the word: Write a word on the board. Choose one student who will guess the word. The rest of the class will describe the word on the board for the student to guess.

Level II

1. Create a crossword puzzle with the words and their meanings.
2. Create sentences with the words to ensure students understand the meaning of each word.

3. Create a word map - examples here http://www.readingrockets.org/strategies/word_maps/.
4. For new words, have students try to 'guess' the meaning of the word before looking it up?
5. Guess the word: Write a word on the board. Choose one student who will guess the word. The rest of the class will describe the word on the board for the student to guess.

Writing Exercise: Friendship – Assign students to write a 500 to 800-word essay on the topic of friendship. What does it mean to you? What makes a friendship strong and lasting? How do you nurture a friendship? What happens when a friendship ends?

Note ⇨ The teacher may choose to provide students with the document, A Quick Grammar Review, found in the Teacher Tool Kit (D).

Level I Quiz

1. What is the Spring Formal and whys is it an important event for the students?

    (a) It is a social event where students gather to party.
    (b) A talent show
    (c) A celebration for the graduating class
    (d) None of the above

2. With the Spring Formal approaching, why was Tamika on edge?

    (a) Dee was nervous so that made Tamika even more nervous.
    (b) Tamika had not completed her religion paper and note cards.
    (c) Dee and Tamika were struggling with their performance song.
    (d) None of the above

3. Tamika began to feel down and nervous about the performance because:

    (a) Tamika did not think the producer would show up.
    (b) Tamika wondered why a producer would want to hear her sing.
    (c) If the producer did not come, all her hard work would be in vain.
    (d) All the above

4. Why was Dee disappointed to see Aminah still at home when they got back from the hair appointments to get ready for the formal?

    (a) Dee wanted the house to herself as she got ready for the formal.
    (b) Dee wanted to rehearse with Tamika but didn't like singing in front of Aminah.
    (c) Dee did not want Aminah to ruin her fun as she got ready for the formal with scolds, warnings or Islamic reminders.
    (d) All the above

5. Why was Aminah still at the apartment when Tamika and Dee returned?

    (a) She wanted to persuade Dee not to go to the formal.
    (b) Aminah lost her research paper and had to re-type it.
    (c) She was late heading out.
    (d) None of the above

True or False

1. Dee often resorts to laughing and joking when she feels under pressure. _____
2. Aminah decided to stay out of Dee's life and worry about her own soul. _____
3. Tamika was angry that Dee felt obligated to explain herself to Aminah. _____
4. The Spring Formal was more important to Dee than it was for Tamika _____
5. Aminah believes maybe her friendship with Dee was not a true friendship _____
6. The song they performed that night was about friendships lost _____
7. Aminah enjoined sleeping in the empty apartment alone _____

8. Aminah admitted she was jealous of Durrah and Tamika's friendship _____
9. Aminah decided to push even harder to win back Durrah's friendship _____
10. Many people have come back to the religion by God guiding them through a loving and patient friend _____

Level II Essay Questions

1. What would success at the Spring Formal mean for Tamika and Dee? Explain your answer.
2. What did Aminah miss most about her friendship with Durrah? Why?
3. How does Aminah plan to rekindle her friendship with Durrah? Do you think it will work? Explain your answer.
4. Have you ever felt like you lost a friend? What emotions did you feel? How did you handle the loss? Were you able to rekindle your friendship with that person? If so, how? If not, what would you have done differently?
5. What does Dee and Tamika's song mean to you? Explain your answer.

Chapter Fourteen

1. **Discussion:** Aminah allows herself a few minutes of rest before getting back to her paper. Have students describe her environment and what she is doing to relax.

   ### Talking Points:
   – She sips a hot cup of honey sweetened peppermint tea.

   – She sits in the quiet kitchen.

   – She ignores the phone ringing, determined not to be interrupted from her moment of relaxation.

   – The sun brightened up the room overpowering the lights in the apartment.

   > Divulge
   > Dynamic
   > Janazah
   > Implication
   > Barzakh
   > Cherubic
   > Oblivious
   > Satiating
   > Carnal
   > Ambiguous
   > Recompense

2. **Discussion:** Aminah is interrupted by a knock at the door. What is her initial response and why does she eventually open it? Have students describe what happens next.

   ### Talking Points:
   – She thinks it might be Dee and Tamika returning early.

   – She remembers they have keys or perhaps they forgot their keys.

   – The knock becomes more forceful which makes her think it is someone else and that something is urgent.

   – She finds Megan at the door holding a newspaper that she nervously rolls up and puts under her arms.

   – Megan forces a smile but it is evident by the expression on her face that her mind is somewhere else.

   – Megan asks if Tamika is home. When Aminah tells her that Tamika and Dee won't return until Sunday, Megan looks away ashamed.

   – Megan realizes Aminah does not know what has happened and proceeds to tell her about the accident that claims the life of Dee and injures Tamika.

   – Megan gives her the newspaper. She hesitates then leaves after not knowing what else to say or do.

3. **Discussion:** Aminah is unwilling to believe that Durrah is dead. What emotions are going through her mind?

   ### Talking Points:
   – She is in shock.

   – She thinks that there must have been a mistake.

   – Echoes of Dee saying "We'll be sashaying past in a few hours" runs through her head.

   – Aminah wants to believe it is a mistake because she has hopes of winning her friend back. She wants to show Durrah the way back to Islam using wisdom and kindness. She wants to have time to do all the things they did as children growing up.

   – She unrolls the paper to read it, checking the date to make sure it is not a hoax.

– She thinks that someone from home would have called to tell her if something had happened only to remember someone had called many times that morning and once the night before but she did not answer the phone.

4. **Discussion:** The word Janazah had never meant much to Aminah except that it was a word in a book. Why does the word sting her heart now?

   ## Talking Points:
   – She learned about it years ago as a child.
   – As a child, she did not understand its implication, meaning or enormity.
   – She only knew that it meant a funeral would be held for a Muslim.
   – She even attended one but had not understood then because the person was a stranger.
   – Aminah felt sickened of her immaturity as she remembered how she stared at the clock the whole time, not wanting to be there.
   – Now she would have to attend the Janazah of her friend.

5. **Discussion:** Angels. Have students describe how Aminah viewed angels as a child. What does she know about them now?

   ## Talking Points:
   – As a child Aminah thought angels were nice, gentle, human-like creatures who resembled a beautiful white woman or cherubic child, adorned with dove-like wings.
   – They appeared only in a person's life to bring them good.
   – They were always smiling, always glowing with happiness, and ever bringing joy by their mere presence.
   – As an adult Aminah knows that angels are not always bringers of glad tidings.
   – Each angel has a different role to fulfill, a different responsibility.
   – They were not human or even human-like.
   – They were created out of light and always obedient to God.
   – Some are in charge of seizing the souls of humans at death.

6. **Discussion:** How does the death of Durrah affect Aminah spiritually?

   ## Talking Points:
   – She is concerned about the state of Dee's soul when she died.
   – She remembers death is the very reason that Muslims live.
   – Every moment in a Muslim's life is in preparation of one's death.
   – Every prayer, every word, every breath was spent hoping that one's soul would be taken in the state of Islam.
   – She finally remembers to say 'inna lillahi wa ilayhi rajioon' though she is ashamed that it took her so long after hearing about Durrah's death.

7. **Discussion:** Barzakh – the barrier – entrapped, is the first part of the journey after death. Have students recount the description in the prophetic Hadith of what happens to a disbeliever when he dies and enters the hereafter.

   ## Talking Points:
   - Stern and harsh angels come to him with black faces and a sack-cloth from Hell.
   - The angels will sit around; the angel of death will sit at his head and will command the soul to come out to the anger and wrath of God.
   - The soul will be dragged out of the body with as much difficulty of pronged skewer being pulled through wet wool.
   - All of the angels will curse the disbelieving soul; it will stink and the angels will put it in the sack-cloth.
   - The cursed soul will not be allowed to go near the gates of heaven or its inhabitants.
   - When asked, it will be announced who the evil soul is, using the worst names with which it was addressed in the world.
   - The soul's book will be registered in 'Sijjin' in the lowest earth.
   - The soul will be returned to his grave and then two angels will come to question him about his Lord, his religion and the messenger of Allah.
   - The cursed soul will not be able to answer the question so his grave will be filled with the heat of hell fire and his grave will become constricted until his ribs are crushed.
   - His deeds will come to him in the form of an ugly man badly dressed with a foul stench.
   - He will be beaten with a rod that will turn him into dust but God will restore his form so that he may be beaten again.
   - He will emit a scream that all of creation can hear except men and jinn.

8. **Discussion:** What is the significance of Aminah's memory of the "sand flying on a windy day?" Have students summarize what happened that day and what this memory represents.

   ## Talking Points:
   - Durrah and Aminah were playing in a sand box watching sand being carried away by the wind. They giggled innocently as they watched it fly away.
   - Leaving Islam was like holding a fistful of sand and letting go.
   - Each sand grain represents a good deed of the Muslim.
   - The brisk wind is the consequences of disbelief.
   - The wind quickly carries away the sand leaving the hand bare.
   - A life of work, of sacrifice, of good works, all rendered useless.
   - Even if you lived a life of Islam, it would benefit you nothing if Islam were absent at death.
   - It does not matter how you lived, it matters how you die.

9. **Discussion:** Aminah is conflicted as to whether she should ask Allah to forgive Durrah? Why does she feel this way?

Talking Points:

– She wondered if Durrah died in the state of Islam.

– She had not seen Durrah prostrate for months.

– She wanted to believe Durrah was just a sinner for which one can pray Allah would forgive her sins.

– But something eerie pricked her senses, taunted her heart.

Vocabulary List:

Divulge - *verb* make known to the public information that was previously known only to a few people or that was meant to be kept a secret

Dynamic - *adj.* characterized by action or forcefulness or force of personality; of or relating to dynamics;

Janazah - *noun* a funeral; a prayer held when a Muslim dies

Implication - *noun* a relation implicated by virtue of involvement or close connection (especially an incriminating involvement); something that is inferred (deduced or entailed or implied); a meaning that is not expressly stated but can be inferred

Barzakh - *noun* an Arabic word that means barrier; a place where souls go to wait for judgment day

Cherubic - *adj.* having a sweet nature befitting an angel or cherub

Oblivious - *adj.* (followed by `to' or `of') lacking conscious awareness of; failing to keep in mind

Satiating - *verb* to satisfy fully or to excess.

Carnal - *adj.* of or relating to the body or flesh; marked by the appetites and passions of the body

Ambiguous - *adj.* having more than one possible meaning; having no intrinsic or objective meaning; open to two or more interpretations; or (often) intended to mislead

Recompense - *noun* the act of compensating for service or loss or injury; payment or reward (as for service rendered); *verb* make payment to; compensate; make amends for; pay compensation for.

Level I

1. Create a word search.
2. Define It! Have students look up the words in a dictionary.
3. Create sentences with the words found from the dictionary.
4. Vocabulary: Unscramble the words.
5. Create a word map (examples here http://www.readingrockets.org/strategies/word_maps/).
6. Guess the word: Write a word on the board. Choose one student who will guess the word. The rest of the class will describe the word on the board for the student to guess.

Level II

1. Create a crossword puzzle with the words and their meanings.
2. Create sentences with the words to ensure students understand the meaning of each word.
3. Create a word map (examples here http://www.readingrockets.org/strategies/word_maps/).
4. For new words, have students try to 'guess' the meaning of the word before looking it up?
5. Guess the word: Write a word on the board. Choose one student who will guess the word. The rest of the class will describe the word on the board for the student to guess.

Level I Quiz

1. Why did Aminah decided to ignore all phone calls Friday night and Saturday morning?
2. How did Aminah take the news of Durrah's death?
3. How did Durrah die?
4. What does Janazah mean?
5. Describe the word 'Barzakh.
6. What are angels and what are they created out of?
7. Why is Aminah hesitant to pray behind Durrah's body at the mosque?
8. Why is Aminah concerned about the state of Durrah's soul?
9. What are the consequences of someone leaving Islam?
10. What dua does Aminah say as she makes her way to the mosque for Durrah's janazah?
11. What are the three questions the angels will ask the inhabitant of the grave?

True or False

1. Aminah ignored the phone calls because she was tired of talking and wanted to relax. _____
2. Megan does not show Aminah much empathy when she tells Aminah about the accident. ____
3. Aminah was too shocked to cry. _____
4. Aminah is unsure whether to pray for Durrah. _____
5. It does not matter how one dies, it matters how they lived. _____
6. Angels have specific duties that they carry out without protest or question. _____
7. Non-Muslim children who die are questioned in the grave. _____
8. People who knew Durrah 'Dee' were shocked that she was a Muslim. _____
9. Aminah and her mother followed the crowd to the burial grounds. _____
10. Aminah's final memory of Durrah as a child is discussing the questioning in the grave. ____

Level II Essay Questions

1. What thoughts and emotions go through Aminah's mind after the news of her friend's death? If you could only choose one word, which word would describe her reaction?
2. Aminah is greatly bothered by people calling Durrah 'Dee'. Explain her displeasure.
3. What is the significance of the memory of "sand flying on a windy day?" Explain.
4. What is the dua that Aminah says as she is driven to the mosque for Durrah's janazah? What is the importance of this dua? Explain your answer.
5. Leaving Islam is like holding a fistful of sand being blown away. What does the sand represent? What does the wind represent? (sand = good deeds, wind = consequences of disbelief)
6. Based on the prophetic Hadith, describe what will happen to the disbeliever when he dies.
7. Some may consider Aminah as being judgmental because all she worries about is whether Durrah died as a Muslim? As a friend and Muslim, should she care about the state of Durrah's soul? Do you agree or disagree? Explain your answer.

Chapter Fifteen

1. **Discussion:** Describe the atmosphere back at the campus apartments where Aminah lives.

   Talking Points:
   - The night is cool with a gentle breeze.
   - The usually rowdy bunch of students is quiet, like muffled whispers behind closed doors.
   - Aminah opened her sliding doors to get fresh air.
   - Her soft voice rang strong, filling the apartment, inviting others to join, to share her feelings, to share in her prayer.

   > Penetrate
   > Encompass
   > Wayward
   > Avert
   > Abode
   > Supplication
   > Orthodox
   > Precaution

2. **Discussion:** Aminah spent half an hour on her prayer. Why?

   Talking Points:
   - She spent extra time reciting and reflecting on the ayahs she recited in her prayer.
   - She spent extra time in prostration as her heart filled with humility and hope.
   - She made supplication after supplication, praying for her soul and the souls of her family, praying that none would go astray.

2. **Discussion:** Aminah does not care that others think it is "uncool" or "unappealing" to be a Muslim. Ask students to explain why she feels this way.

   Talking Points:
   - Life is too short to care about what others think about you and your faith.
   - Death can come at any time.
   - We are held accountable to Allah for all that we say and do in this life.
   - We will be questioned about our actions and belief or lack thereof when we die.

3. **Discussion:** Aminah contemplates the spiritual state of Muslims today. How they view and implement faith in their lives? What are her conclusions?

   Talking Points:
   - The words of Allah are trivial to them when compared to their life of wealth, status and petty desires.
   - The lives of Muslims today bear little resemblance to the Muslims of old.
   - Islam is a source of shame instead of pride.
   - Muslims seek to find an identity other than Islam.
   - Muslims were weak in faith, lacked belief in the Hereafter causing them to abandon their religion and replace it with foreign ideas.

- Muslims seek to render themselves free from having to teach Islam as the only path to heaven and free from practicing it themselves.

4. **Discussion:** What is it that Muslims lack today?

   ## Talking Points:
   – They lack sincerity in their faith and actions.
   – They lack dedication and commitment to their religion.
   – They lack faith itself; Islam is missing from their lives.

5. **Discussion:** What causes a Muslim to abandon the truth? What caused Dee to abandon her faith?

   ## Talking Points:
   – They often prefer the life of ignorance, the life of ease and no obligation to God or His religion; Durrah was getting tired of the strict laws imposed in Islam because it placed an obstacle in the way of her desires.
   – Weakness of faith; often they believe, but the temptations of the worldly life is too strong. Durrah no doubt had faith and knew the truth but the desires of this world were a far greater temptation.
   – Lack of faith in the hereafter; when one does not keep the remembrance of the hereafter, its punishments, its rewards, he forgets and falls easily to the temptations of this world.

6. **Discussion:** Tamika returns home late that night. Aminah observes her for a bit knowing she has been through a lot. Have students describe her appearance and disposition when she first enters the room.

   ## Talking Points:
   – She appeared weak.
   – She was tired and pale.
   – Her hair was pulled back but slightly disheveled.
   – She still had her hospital wristband on her wrist and bandage that covered where her IV had been.
   – She walked slowly and appeared older than when Aminah last saw her.
   – She sat silently staring out the window into the dark.

7. **Discussion:** Tamika had not known about Dee's death until after she was released from the hospital. Why was that? How did she find out?

   ## Talking Points:
   – The hospital workers did not want her visitor to tell her until later, probably after they knew she would be okay.
   – Perhaps the shock of her friend's death would be too much for her.
   – When she was finally released, her friend Makisha told her about Dee's death.
   – Makisha took Tamika to the school chapel for a program dedicated to Dee.

8. **Discussion:** During the program dedicated for Dee, everyone was moved to tears as they remembered Dee. Why do you think they were crying: Kevin, Makisha, audience and Tamika?

   ### Talking Points:
   - Kevin loved Dee; he was intending to marry her and even raise a family with her hoping that one day they would both become better Muslims.
   - Makisha covered her face with sadness and shame; perhaps out of guilt for the way she treated Dee and her attitude toward her.
   - The speeches, music and clips of Dee and her performances moved the audience to tears in awe of her.
   - Tamika remembered what Dee was doing before the accident, singing and being silly.
   - Tamika also knew that for Dee, returning back to her faith was no longer an option; Dee did not have a chance to do right by her faith and seek God's forgiveness.

9. **Discussion:** Dee's death was the catalyst that pushed Tamika to do what she had wanted to do since the first moment she learned about Islam, to become a Muslim. Have students discuss why they think that is?

   ### Talking Points:
   - She realized that death could take her at any time, like it took Dee, without warning or a chance to repent.
   - Life is short and no one knows when death will come for them.
   - She did not want to die as a disbeliever.
   - Dee had always said she would return to Islam later in her life but her life ended before she could do it.
   - Tamika was afraid that if she pursued her dreams of stardom she ran the chance of ending up like Dee, knowing the truth but not accepting it and implementing it.

10. **Discussion:** In Tamika's conclusion during her presentation, she explains why she chose Islam as her religion. Have students summarize her conclusion of Islam.

    ### Talking Points:
    - Islam is the fastest growing religion.
    - Its roots reach far back to the time of Adam.
    - It is a holistic religion, its teachings affecting every aspect of the Muslim's life.
    - Islam holds an authenticity that other religions do not due to the fact that its followers adhere strictly to the original teachings.
    - Islam is the only religion in its orthodox form.

11. **Discussion:** have students describe Tamika's transformation after embracing Islam.

    ### Talking Points:
    - She begins to cover.

- She memorizes Qur'an.
- She gives up public singing.
- She continues writing songs, her newfound faith being the subject of many of them.
- Her new goal is to one day sing her songs for Muslim women.

Vocabulary List:

Penetrate - *verb* come to understand; pass into or through, often by overcoming resistance; become clear or enter one's consciousness or emotions

Encompass - *verb* include in scope; include as part of something broader

Wayward - *adj.* resistant to guidance or discipline

Avert - *verb* turn away or aside; prevent the occurrence of; prevent from happening

Abode - *noun* housing that someone is living in; any address at which you dwell more than temporarily

Supplication - *noun* a humble request for help from someone in authority; a prayer asking God's help

Orthodox - *adj.* adhering to what is commonly accepted;

Precaution - *noun* a precautionary measure warding off impending danger or damage or injury etc.; the trait of practicing caution in advance; judiciousness in avoiding harm or danger

Level I

1. Create a word search.
2. Define It! Have students look up the words in a dictionary.
3. Create sentences with the words found from the dictionary.
4. Vocabulary: Unscramble the words.
5. Create a word map (examples here: http://www.readingrockets.org/strategies/word_maps/).
6. Guess the word: Write a word on the board. Choose one student who will guess the word. The rest of the class will describe the word on the board for the student to guess.

Level II

1. Create a crossword puzzle with the words and their meanings.
2. Create sentences with the words to ensure students understand the meaning of each word.
3. Create a word map (examples here http://www.readingrockets.org/strategies/word_maps/).
4. For new words, have students try to 'guess' the meaning of the word before looking it up?
5. Guess the word: Write a word on the board. Choose one student who will guess the word. The rest of the class will describe the word on the board for the student to guess.

Level I Quiz

1. What was the last thing Tamika remembered Dee doing before the accident?
2. What was the last thing Tamika remembered before waking up in the hospital?
3. Why did the hospital keep Tamika?
4. Where did the school hold its memorial service for Dee?
5. What is it that Muslims lack today? Why are they so unsuccessful?
6. How did Aminah spend her evening?
7. How did each verse affect Aminah's heart as she recited it in her prayer?
8. What is the Day of Judgment?
9. Why did Tamika finally decide to go ahead and become a Muslim?
10. Why is submission after death not accepted
11. Why did Tamika choose Islam for herself?

Level II Essay Questions

1. Summarize Tamika's journey to Islam. Mention her struggles and obstacles and what finally pushed her to take the final step of converting.
2. Was there a benefit to Tamika delaying her conversion until when she did? What was good? What was bad? Explain your answers.
3. "Words can't describe me" Dee once said. In your own words, explain why this sentence rings true for Dee.
4. Do you think Dee's death is what finally convinced Tamika to convert? Explain your answer.
5. If Dee had survived, do you think she would have changed any aspects of her life? Explain your answer.
6. How often do you think about death? Does it serve as a reminder? How does it make you feel? Does it cause you to change any views or aspects in your life? Does it change your attitude about faith and obedience to God?

Final Assignment: Assign the students to write a book review for *If I Should Speak*.

Provide Level I students with a copy of Level I Book Review Guide found in the Teacher's Tool Kit (G).

Provide Level II students with a copy of Level II Book Review Guide found in the Teacher's Tool Kit (H).

Teacher Tool Kit

Book Character Descriptions

Tamika Douglass – a black/African-American Christian, 18 year old. Her family lives in Milwaukee, Wisconsin. She has an older sister and brother who are twins. Tamika does journal writing. She wants to be a professional singer, but her family wants her to attend and graduate from the university. She would rather continue to write songs and begin a singing career. She has an older sister and brother who are twins.

Jennifer Mayer – Tamika's white roommate. She has long blonde hair and blue eyes. Jennifer is slovenly, refusing to do her share of housekeeping chores. She is also a liar and a racist.

Makisha – Tamika's best black Christian girlfriend, 18 years old, and their families have known each other for many years. Makisha's uncle is a Christian preacher. Makisha is also attending the university.

Dr. Sanders – a black/African-American, originally from Tampa Bay, Florida and he is a USA citizen. He teaches Religion courses at the university. He was a member of Tamika's Conduct Board. He believes in God and tries to take the good from all without being a member of any organized religion. He doesn't believe that Jesus is God.

Durrah "Dee" Gonzalez – 19 years old and a junior at the university. Her family is Hispanic-and originates from Cuba. She and her family live in Atlanta, Georgia. Dee's family consists of her parents, four girls and three boys. Dee is a tall, slender woman with wavy, dark long hair. She is a strong-minded young lady, and has won several academic awards and almost every beauty contest she had entered. She has a lovely singing voice and wants to have a professional career as a singer. She describes herself as a Muslim but considers herself lazy where her practice of Islam is concerned. She knows Islam is right but it conflicts with her goal of being a professional singer. Aminah is her childhood best friend.

Aminah Ali – 18 years old and grew up in Atlanta, Georgia. She is already a junior at the university. She's a strict practicing Muslim. She considers herself to be black as her dad's half black, and her my mom is white. Amina is upset about the way Dee is mixing with the opposite sex, missing prayers and joking about Islam.

Sulayman Ali – Aminah's brother. He is also attending the university and is well-known for his regular editorial column in the university newspaper. He writes "controversial" articles, which in Dee's opinion were no more than him expressing the strong moral views that he had as a Muslim.

Reference List

Quotations from the Bible Scripture taken from *The Holy Bible, New International Version* ®. Copyright © 1973, 1984 by International Bible Society. Used by permission of Zondervan Publishing House.

Quotations from the Qur'an are taken from Yusuf Ali translations.

The Holy Qur'an; Al-'Ankaboot, 29:64

Al-A'raaf, 7:172-3

Ali Imraan, 3:42-60

Al-Araaf, 7:2-3

An-Nisaa, 4:171

Al-Maa'idah, 5:17

ibid, 5:18

Philips, p. 46

Al-Aqeedah at Tahaaweeyah, (5th ed. 1972), p.273, cited in Fundamentals of Tawheed; p.49.

Darussalam Publishers, p.27

John 4:48

Ali Imran, 3:49

John 7:16

Ibid, 8:42-43

Ibid, 5:30

Numbers, 23:19

Ali Imran, 3:60

Ibid, 3:85

Ibid, 3:31

Ibid, 3:91

Ash-Shoora, 42:32

Al-A'raaf, 7:40

Al-A'raaf, 7:40

Al-Hajj, 22:31

Glossary

Arabic – English

As-salaamu-alaikum - Peace be upon you," the standard Muslim greeting. Muslim response is "Wa-'alaikum-as-salaam"

Khimaar - a head covering worn by a Muslim woman that covers her entire head and neck and is drawn over her bosom area, exposing only her face.

Wudhu - referring to the ablution which is washing in preparation of prayer.

The symbol (s) is an abbreviation of the Arabic statement that translates to mean, "Prayers and peace be upon him," which a Muslim says at each mention of the Prophet's name out of respect for him.

Alhamdulillaah - All praises are due to God alone.

MashaAllaah - A common Arabic termed used by Muslims in response to hearing some news; the term literally means, "It was God's will." hoping that one's soul would be taken while he or she was in the state of Islam.

sallaahu'alayhi wa salaam - May prayers and peace be upon him.

Dhikr - Literally, to remember God, but in this context it means to recite the name of God repeatedly using various praiseworthy terms.

Dunya - anything that pertains to the present world as opposed to the Hereafter.

Shaytaan - Satan

Riba - Usury

Halaal - permissible

Tahajjud - The voluntary night prayer, best when prayed in the last third of the night before dawn.

du'aa - Informal supplication to God for something one wants.

inshaAllah - God-willing

da'wah - An Arabic term meaning to teach someone about Islam.

Ayaat al-Kursee - The verse of the Footstool" (2:255), traditionally recited by Muslims before going to bed.

Bismillaah - In the name of God

Hijab - The Muslim women's Islamic covering of her head and body.

Inna lillaahi wa inna ilayhi raji'oon - From God we come, and unto Him is our return.

Barzakh - the Barrier—entrapped. And there was no turning back—the first part of the journey to Heaven—or Hell.

English

Born Again Christian - a label used by some protestant Christian denominations (churches) for non-practicing Christians who admit publically to being a sinner, who then ask for forgiveness from Jesus, state they believe in the Trinity and profess their belief that Jesus died on the cross so their sins can be forgiven and they can then be allowed into heaven (Jannah). Christians believe that only people who profess this belief in Jesus as Savior can get into heaven. Catholic Christians do not incorporate this label into their practice. The Catholic Church requires 'sinners' to make a private confession of their sins to a priest and then ask the priest to obtain forgiveness for them. Catholics are required to make confessions on a regular basis.

Islam - means submission or surrender.

Shahadah - acceptance of Islam:
"I bear witness that none has the right to be worshipped but God alone. And I bear witness that Muhammad is the Messenger of God."

Backbiting - to gossip or tell negative things about another person.

Quick Grammar and Writing Tips

Resources:

– The book titled *Star Writers* authored by Amatullah Al-Marwani

– Basic sentence and grammar review:
   http://grammar.about.com/od/basicsentencegrammar/u/grammarlabel.htm

ESL:

– Internet web site for reviewing Grammar–ESL Student: http://esl.about.com/

– Diagraming sentences: The practice of diagraming is helpful for people who need to visualize an idea in order to grasp it. Refer to:
http://opinionator.blogs.nytimes.com/2012/06/18/taming-sentences/?ref=opinion

Keep a sharp eye out for repeated words used often in student sentences. Remind students to use a 'thesaurus' to vary adjectives.

Instead of using short sentences show the students how to connect them. Connecting sentences takes practice and there's never any one right answer. Students can use words like "and," "or," "but," "however," "because," "although," "and maybe then," "as," "thus," "if," et cetera. Students can also use punctuation like commas (,), colons (:), semicolons (;), dashes (—), ellipsis (…), and parenthesis (( )).

Homonyms - Misuse of homonyms is also a common grammar error. Words that sound the same, are spelled differently, and have a different meaning. Common Homonyms:

know/no	hour/our	forth/fourth	complement/compliment
its/it's	flair/flare	carat/carrot	emigrate/immigrate
bases/basis	capital/capitol	coarse/course	peak/pique/peek
read/red	lead/led	cite/sight/site	incidence/incidents
faze/phase	tea/tee	ensure/insure	imminent/eminent
wrack/rack	hardy/hearty	tour/tore	stationary/stationery
board/bored	break/brake	elicit/illicit	rain/rein/reign
I'll/aisle/isle	allowed/aloud	who's/whose	principal/principle
whole/hole	chord/cord	pour/poor/pore	naval/navel
descent/dissent	role/roll	sense/since	premier/premiere
racket/racquet	heir/err	scene/seen	palate/palette/pallet
weather/whether	trooper/trouper	ate/eight	there/their/they're
piece/peace	brows/browse	by/bye/buy	

Antonyms - words with an opposite meaning to another word:
   white-black, up-down, right-wrong, fast-slow, day-night, tall-short, big-little, hot-cold

Synonyms – same or equivalent meaning: silent-quite, fun-enjoy, hard-tough

Matching Noun and Verb - Singular versus Plural

    Examples:

        Khalid *writes* wonderful poetry. (singular)

        Maryam and Amel are learning to *write* poetry. (plural)

        Samuel *was* late for class. (singular)

        Saba and Amatullah *were* late for class. (plural)

        He *is* going to study for a math test. (singular)

        They *are* studying for a math test. (plural)

Articles - When to use *a* or *an*

    http://esl.about.com/od/beginningenglish/ig/Basic-English/Articles.htm

        Use the word *an* when it is before a word that begins with a vowel (a-e-i-o-u)

        She ate *an* apple every day. Jamilah was *an* excellent student.

        Use the word a when it is before a word that begins with all letters except a-e-i-o-u.

        They bought *a* bag of chips to eat with their hamburgers.

Adverbs and Adjectives

    Adjectives are placed directly before a noun. They are words that describe:

        I bought a *comfortable* chair.

        Amel chose *black* shoes and *black* socks to wear with her *dark blue* abeya.

        Jacob is a *popular* name chosen for *male* babies in 2011.

    Adverbs are easily recognized because they end in 'ly'. Adverbs are often used at the end of a sentence to modify the verb (Jack *drove* carelessly).

Nouns - people, places or things.

Pronouns - may be used in place of nouns: we, I, they, them, his, her, she and him.

Verbs - action words such as jumped, run, sailing, writing, baking, reading, etc.

Islamic Fiction Definition and Fiction Writing Review

Source: Islamic Fiction Books blog site at: www.islamicfictionbooks.wordpress.com

What is Islamic Fiction?

Islamic Fiction refers to creative, imaginative, and non-preachy fiction literature written by Muslims who intend for readers to learn something positive about Islam and benefit from reading an Islamic fiction story. Islamic fiction incorporates religious content and themes in the stories and may include non-fictionalized historical or factual Islamic content with or without direct reference to the Qur'an or the Sunnah. Islamic fiction may also include modern, real life situations and moral dilemmas.

Islamic Fiction does not include 'Harmful Content': vulgar language, sexually explicit content, unIslamic practices that are not identified as unIslamic, or content that portrays Islam in a negative way.

Please Note - Differences in Islamic Practices and Teachings

While Islamic knowledge presented in Islamic Fiction may be taken directly from the Holy Qur'an and traditions of the Prophet Muhammad (peace be upon him), as well as from Islamic history, not all of the Islamic content in these books will be considered factual or acceptable by all Muslim readers. This is due to differences between a Muslim reader and the writers, editors, and publishers with respect to personal practices, beliefs and knowledge, as well as the influence of his mathab, culture, and tradition.

Islamic Reminder

Determining the accuracy and permissibility of Islamic content is the responsibility of every adult Muslim reader. This may differ according to individual differences in madhab and practice. All Muslim parents, guardians, teachers, and school administrators must determine whether a book's content is halal for their children and students. This Islamic Reminder holds true for all materials a Muslim reads.

Fiction Writing Review

Resource: The book titled *Star Writers* authored by Amatullah Al-Marwani
Every story has a beginning, a middle (turning point), and an ending.

Antagonists - the villains of the story.

Antonym - a word that has the opposite meaning of another word in the same language.

Characters - Characters are the people or animate objects moving the narrative along—things happen to them, with them, because of them, in spite of them, and all around them.

Climax - ending of the story, high point, problem solved, answering the questions of your story. This technique involves spilling the beans, letting the cat out of the bag, showing your cards…basically resolving the problem(s) your Islamic story has been leading up to.

Creative Plot - ups, downs, twists, turns, surprises, and climaxes. The *story* consists of the events which occur, while the *plot* is the sequence in which the writer arranges those events.

Details - what help your readers to "see" the characters and settings you create for them with your writing.

Dialogue - the speech of the characters in your story.

Ending Story - Remember, these last lines are the final experience readers will take away when they leave the world you've created for them. Make it count and then move on to writing your next Islamic story!

First Person - first person point of view or *voice* refers to using words like "I, me, mine, my, we, ours, us."

Five Senses - see, hear, feel, touch and smell

Foreshadowing - giving away clues or *foreshadowing* along the way will keep the reader guessing and thinking about what happens next. (hints)

Foreword - the introductory section at the beginning of a book, which may be written by the author of the book, but is often by someone else.

Genre - \zhän'ra\ (from Old French meaning "kind" or "type"): a category of writing, recognizable by a unique style, form, or content ~ *Because of her love for horses, she preferred to read books in the genres of nature and animals.*

Homophone - are words that sound alike but are spelled differently and have different meanings such as: lie (lye?) in wait (weight?), ready to bear (bare?) down on you (ewe?) like prey (pray?) if you've shown (shone?) any careless instants (instance?) in your (you're?) writing!

Manuscript - a copy or original, usually typed or computer printed, of a literary work that is submitted to a publisher.

Metaphor - A *metaphor* compares two things but in a direct way, without the use of "like" or "as." Insha'Allah, your Islamic story is a shining star! And, insha'Allah, you'll be a busy beaver working on your next one before you know it!

Protagonists - are the heroes of the story.

Simile - a *simile* is a way of comparing two things using "like" or "as." Insha'Allah, your Islamic story will shine like a star! And, Insha'Allah, you'll be as busy as a beaver working on your next one before you know it!

Story Line - ups and downs not a straight line

Synonym - is a word (or phrase) that has the same meaning as another word (or phrase) in the same language.

Syntax - is linking verbiage correctly into an orderly sentence structure according to grammatical outlines and comprehensive cohesion. In other words, it's writing right!

Tags - dialogue tags tell us which character is "it"— in other words, who's talking. The most common dialogue tag is the word "said."

Tense - Stories, like life, take place in time, either the present tense, the past tense, or the future tense.

Third Person - third person point of view or voice refers to using words like "he, she, it, his, hers, they, them, their, theirs."

Turning Point - leading to the Turning Point involves revealing the story, piece by piece, with just enough excitement to keep your readers involved.

Recommended Reading List

Level 1 and II Students

Jesus Prophet of Islam
authored by Muhammad 'Ata ur-Rahim and revised by co-author Ahmad Thomson

What Islam Is All About
authored by Yahiya Emerick

A Voice: The Sequel to If I Should Speak
authored by Umm Zakiyyah

Footsteps
authored by Umm Zakiyyah

Hearts We Lost
authored by Umm Zakiyyah

Realities of Submission
authored by Umm Zakiyyah

Echoes series: *Echoes, Rebounding, Turbulence, Ripples,* and *Silence*
authored by Jamilah Kolocotronis

The Size of a Mustard Seed
authored by Umm Juwayriyah

Sophia's Journal: Time Warp 1857
authored by Najiyah Diana Helwani

Islamic Rose Books series:
The Visitors, Hijab-EZ Friends, Stories, Saying Goodbye, and *Reunion*
authored by Linda D. Delgado

From Somalia, with Love
authored by Na'ima B Robert

Boy vs Girl
authored by Na'ima B. Robert

Isabella: A Girl of Muslim Spain
authored by Yahiya Emerick

Level I Book Review Guide

Level I Assignment – Written Book Review of *If I Should Speak*

Instructions: Review and answer the questions listed below. Use your answers to form a basis for writing a book review. Your written review should be at minimum one page in length.

1. Does the title seem appropriate for the story?
2. At the end of each chapter, is there a hook or transition?
3. Has the author introduced characters effectively?
4. Does the author present the physical details of the characters in order to provide a clear visual image?
5. Are the characters realistic and believable?
6. Are complications introduced in the story?
7. Does the author's writing paint a picture?
8. Is there a good balance of dialogue and action?
9. Is the dialogue used effectively to create reader empathy and move the plot forward?
10. Is the climax (ending of the story) appropriate?
11. Is the ending satisfying?
12. What did you like most about the story?
13. What didn't you like about the story?
14. Would you recommend this book to others?

Level II Book Review Guide

Level II Assignment – Written Book Review of *If I Should Speak*

Instructions: Review and answer the questions listed below. Use your answers to form a basis for writing a book review. Your written review should be at minimum one page in length.

Hook

Does the title seem appropriate for the story or subject matter?

Did the first three paragraphs in Chapter 1 draw you into the story?

At the end of each chapter, is there a hook or transition?

Does the author use foreshadowing (do the events that have taken place add up to the end resolution)?

Exposition

Has the author introduced characters effectively?

Has the author set a tone for the work?

Is the tone appropriate for the setting of the story?

Does the author state the facts?

Rising Action

Does the action build the content of the work?

Are complications introduced?

Does the action help develop the characters?

Climax

Is there a clear highest point of the action?

Is the climax appropriate given the genre?

Resolution

Does the story have a clear conclusion?

Is the ending satisfying?

Is there a planned series of carefully selected interrelated incidents?

Are the interrelated incidents driven by a struggle between/among opposing forces?

Does each incident result in an appropriate resolution?

Is each incident clearly relevant to the overall storyline?

Does the setting provide a sense of story?

Is the setting appropriate for the story?

Does the setting add to the emotional tension?

Does the writing paint a picture?

Descriptive Details

    Does the author present the physical details of the characters in order to provide a clear visual image?

    Does the author use/describe physical objects relevant to the characters that further the storyline?

Goals and Personal Agenda

    Do the characters have goals and personal agendas?

    If the characters have goals, do they encounter obstacles to those goals?

    Antagonist present?

    Antagonist appropriate?

    Tension between the characters?

Realistic and Believable Characters

    Flawed to provide dimension?

    Are the characters concrete—do they seem real?

    Do you feel compassion for one or more of the characters?

    Was the author able to create like or dislike for his or her characters?

    Are the characters well motivated (emotional motivation)?

    Do the characters have good reasons for their actions (physical reasons)?

    Are all/most of the characters' actions related to the climax and resolution?

    At the end of the book, has the main character changed in some way?

    Are there situations that heighten the conflict?

    Are there turning points in the plot?

    Has the author used action verbs appropriately?

Dialogue Structure

    Does the dialogue/speech of the characters reveal their important traits?

    Is the dialogue conversational and easy to read?

    Is there a good balance of dialogue and action?

Is the Dialogue Used Effectively?

    To create reader empathy?

    To move the plot forward?

    To manipulate the pace?

    To convey the differences between the characters?

    To convey body language?

Is the ending or resolution satisfying to the reader?

Is the ending or resolution appropriate for the story?

Answer Key

Chapter One

Level I Quiz

Multiple Choice
1) D
2) A
3) D
4) D
5) A

True or False
1. F
2. F
3. T
4. T
5. T

Level II – 5 Essay questions: Each answer is worth 1 to 20 points with a total score of 100 points possible for all five questions.

Chapter Two

Level I Quiz

Fill-In answers
1. Repercussions
2. Skeptical
3. Influx
4. Altercation
5. Prejudice and bias and expel
6. Controversial
7. Ablution
8. Stereotype and motive and verdict
9. Judgmental
10. Assault
11. Wudhu
12. Khimaar

Essay answers

1. He wanted to discuss her research paper and course work.
2. Dr. Sanders convinced enough board members that she was not a threat and suggested a lighter sentence of moving her from the shared room with Jennifer.
3. Bias is a tendency to assume a certain viewpoint or answer is correct. Prejudice is a feeling, viewpoint or opinion formed beforehand or without knowledge, thought or reason. Prejudice is often developed when biased ideas are reinforced repeatedly.
4. Dee was popular. She did not look nor acted like a "strict" Muslim.
5. Aminah's complexion gave Tamika the impression she was either Arab or white. Also, Tamika did not think an American would choose to wear Islamic attire.
6. Mocking any part of Islam is considered disbelief and that took a person out of the folds of Islam. A person who leaves Islam could go to the hell fire if they don't repent.

True or False

1. T
2. F
3. F
4. F
5. F

Level II – 5 Essay questions: Each answer is worth 1 to 20 points with a total score of 100 points possible for all five questions.

Chapter Three

Level I Quiz

Word Match

11. Affiliation
12. Monotheism
13. Deduce
14. Insouciant
15. Affable
16. Sentiments
17. fundamentalist
18. Implication
19. Contradictory
20. Delirious

Multiple Choice

1. b) Islam
2. b) Believed Jesus is a prophet not God
3. b) Muslim
4. a) Makisha was envious of Dee's popularity
5. a) The Qur'an

True or False

1. T
2. F
3. F
4. F
5. T

Level II – 5 Essay questions: Each answer is worth 1 to 20 points with a total score of 100 points possible for all five questions.

Chapter Four

Level I Quiz

Essay answers

1. Islam means submission or surrender; it is the submission and surrender to God alone. Muslims do not believe in trinity or a man being God or Son of God.
2. To worship God alone and to obey his prophets.
3. Aminah is respectful and diplomatic; Dee is very critical and laughs at her confusion.
4. Tamika grew up loving the religion from her mother.
5. Dee's mother constantly lectures her; Dee's father would stare at her silently, disapprovingly.
6. They said they would start praying and that they would go to heaven if they are really good Muslims.
7. The person should be calm, diplomatic, sensitive, patient and respectful.
8. Fitrah is the normal nature or instinct of a person. It is used in Islamic law to refer to laws that complement or promote a certain instinct – e.g., the oneness of God.
9. The knowledge if you heard the truth, Islam, while you are alive.
10. Fear, pride, or weakness is one of many reasons people do not accept Islam. Many people choose to stick to the religions of old even after God sent messengers. Followers of Moses did not accept Jesus thus establishing Judaism. Followers of Jesus did not accept Muhammad (pbuh) therefore Christianity remained.

Level II – 5 Essay questions: Each answer is worth 1 to 20 points with a total score of 100 points possible for all five questions.

Chapter Five

Level I Quiz

Essay answers

1. He seemed to make excuses, he fumbled through his answers, he could not give her a concrete acceptable answer, and he gave her contradicting answers.
2. Tamika is beginning to question her faith and Christ. She refuses to "just believe".
3. She believes the girls meant well and the problem would pass.
4. They believe that God is a 'black' man as oppose to Christians who portray Jesus or God as a white man.
5. No one has the answer for her, everyone's answers are different, they tell her not to question, just believe. She is warned against turning her back on Christ.

True or False

F
T
F
T
T
T
T
F
F
T

Level II – 5 Essay questions: Each answer is worth 1 to 20 points with a total score of 100 points possible for all five questions.

Chapter Six

Level I Quiz

Multiple Choice

1. Her mother
2. All of the above
3. They both want to sing professionally
4. All of the above
5. All of the above

True or False

F
F
T
T
T
T
F
T

Level II – 5 Essay questions: Each answer is worth 1 to 20 points with a total score of 100 points possible for all five questions.

Writing Exercise: Assign students to write a short Islamic fiction story. They may choose any genre for their stories. Maximum word count for the story for Level I students is 800 words. Maximum word count for Level II students is 1,200 words. Provide students with a copy of the document – *Islamic Fiction Definition and Fiction Writing Review* found in the Teacher Tool Kit (G).

Chapter Seven

Level I Quiz

Essay answers

1. She is afraid Aminah will tell her parents and she wants to tell them herself.
2. They impose strict rules on Dee, they won't approve of her singing professionally.
3. They would get to have all the fun they wanted and would not have to worry about Aminah reminding Dee of her religious obligations.
4. *Judaism* refers to the followers of Moses (as) who did not accept Jesus.

   Christianity refers to the followers Jesus (as) who accepted the message of Jesus (as) who also later became those who worship him.

   Islam is the religion of Muslims who follow the teaching of Prophet Muhammad (as) as the messenger of Allah.
5. She is worried what her family and friends would say and think. She is not ready to give up everything yet.

True or False

F
T
T
T
F
T
T
F
T

Level II – 5 Essay questions: Each answer is worth 1 to 20 points with a total score of 100 points possible for all five questions.

Chapter Eight

Level I Quiz

Multiple Choice answers

1. b) Sheet
2. a) She is used to non-Muslims displeasure with the Muslim dress.
3. c) God
4. d) All of the above
5. d) All of the above
6. d) All of the above
7. b) She feared what her family and friends would say or how they would look at her.
8. b) Weak
9. a) She was a Muslim and still doing what she wanted.
10. d) All of the above

Level II – 4 Essay questions: Each answer is worth 1 to 25 points with a total score of 100 points possible for all five questions.

Chapter Nine

Level I Quiz

Multiple Choice

1. d) All of the above
2. a) Unique
3. a) The visit was a major part of her assignment.
4. d) All of the above
5. c) She is only there because her mother wants her to be.
6. d) All of the above
7. b) An abiyah
8. b) Because it poses the danger of people misunderstanding the Qur'an since jilbaab is mentioned in the Qur'an.
9. a) Tamika was mesmerized by the unity of the Muslim women. She felt like she belonged in the prayer hall with the praying women.
10. b) Tamika did not know where to look as she is accustomed to looking a person in the face and the veil posed a barrier between them.

Level II – 5 Essay questions: Each answer is worth 1 to 20 points with a total score of 100 points possible for all five questions.

Chapter Ten

Level I Quiz

Essay answers

1. These were not oppressed women. That they had chosen their way of life and no one forced them to cover or convert.
2. She felt dirty, like a heathen and that she was a spectacle in front of the family.
3. After learning about Islam and Muslims from Dee and Aminah's family she learned that all of her views were baseless and that she judged Muslims based on what she was raised to believe.
4. If you around something or someone for too long, their character, behaviors, views and attitudes begin to rub off on you.
5. She did not want to betray her friend.
6. Needed to vent and an understanding ear.
7. Durrah has become more resistant and irritable; she does not talk to her anymore.
8. She takes everything she reads and learns seriously and to heart.

Level II – 5 Essay questions: Each answer is worth 1 to 20 points with a total score of 100 points possible for all five questions.

Writing exercise: Awkward Moments – Assign the students to write a 500-800 word essay describing an awkward moment in their life.

Chapter Eleven

Level I Quiz

Essay answers

1. She rushes to the bathroom feeling sorry for Dee and does not offer to comfort her.
2. She did not know what to say or what to do.
3. At first she is embarrassed but then she just looks away not caring Tamika saw her because she did not know why she was crying.
4. She is strong and a fighter. She is easy-going, always good for a laugh, kind, strived to achieve her dreams despite obstacles in her path, always forgiving and thinking the best of others, looking at the bright side.
5. She made it a regular habit after she read about the immense rewards of praying the Duhaa prayer.
6. In high school they were strong, their faith high, the spearheads of Islamic activities in their school, both observed Islamic attire. Durrah was a lot more confident and outspoken when it came to giving da'wah, Aminah was timid and self-conscious.
7. It was abrupt and unexpected. And that she is capable of being influenced by temptation the same way Dee had.
8. They would deduce that Dee was in need of attention, attention she did not receive at home.
9. Dee and Tamika's friendship is based on mutual understanding of what the other was going through. They each provide a sympathetic ear to the other. They have a lot in common, like singing and wanting to go professional with their singing career, they both have strict parents who do not like their career or life choices.
10. Dee invites Tamika to camping with her and a few friends.

Level II – 5 Essay questions: Each answer is worth 1 to 20 points with a total score of 100 points possible for all five questions.

Chapter Twelve

Level I Quiz

Essay answers

1. It was filled with excitement. It was relaxing and gave her tranquility, peace and a much needed escape from the world.
2. All the camp stories made her afraid of the dark and every movement in the forest.

3. She thinks they will not agree to her marrying him because he is not Muslim.
4. Tamika says to just do it and get it over with. She should let her family meet Kevin.
5. Kevin is mixed with Mexican, Egyptian/white heritages. His grandfather is Muslim and up until his parents divorced, he practiced Islam and even prayed. He and Dee both want to eventually become practicing Muslims and raise their children to be Muslim.

True or False

1. F
2. T
3. T
4. T
5. T

Level II – 5 Essay questions: Each answer is worth 1 to 20 points with a total score of 100 points possible for all five questions.

Chapter Thirteen

Level I Quiz

Multiple Choice

1. (a) It is a social event where students gather to party.
2. (a) Dee was nervous so that made Tamika even more nervous.
3. (d) All the above
4. (c) Dee did not want Aminah to ruin her fun as she got ready for the formal with scolds, warnings or Islamic reminders.
5. (b) Aminah lost her research paper and had to re-type it.

True or False

T
T
T
F
F
F
F
T
F
T

Level II – 5 Essay questions: Each answer is worth 1 to 20 points with a total score of 100 points possible for all five questions.

Writing Exercise: Friendship – Assign students to write a 500 to 800-word essay on the topic of friendship. What does it mean to you? What makes a friendship strong and lasting? How do you nurture a friendship? What happens when a friendship ends?

Chapter Fourteen

Level I Quiz

Essay answers

1. She wanted to finish her paper without any interruptions.
2. She was shocked and in denial. She could not believe it. She felt weak in the legs and needed to sit down.
3. She died in a car accident when a drunk driver struck her car.
4. Janazah means funeral. It is a prayer that is performed before the body is placed it the grave.
5. Barzakh means a barrier. It is a place that the souls go to be questioned by the angels.
6. Angels are creatures without a choice. They are a creation with specific duties that they fulfill without protest or question. They are created out of light.
7. She is concerned that Durrah died in a state of disbelief in Islam.
8. She is worried if Durrah died a Muslim or not because of the grave consequences if she did not.
9. All of their good deeds are erased and they are left bare.
10. Our Lord, let not our hearts deviate now after You have guided us, and grant us mercy from Your presence, for You are the Bestower!
11. Who is your Lord? What is your religion? He will be asked who Prophet Muhammad is.

True or False

1. F
2. T
3. T
4. T
5. F
6. T
7. F
8. T
9. T
10. T

Level II – 7 Essay questions: Each answer is worth 1 to 14 points with a total score of 100 points possible for all five questions.

Chapter Fifteen

Level I Quiz

Essay answers

1. Dee was singing and being silly.
2. She remembered a piercing shrill from Dee as bright lights filled the car and the sudden impact shocking them both.
3. They kept her out of precaution than necessity.
4. At the school's chapel.
5. They lack sincerity, dedication and faith.
6. She spent it praying and supplicating for her and her family.
7. It gave it life, causing her heart to overflow with love, hope and fear of her Lord
8. It is the day when all will be judged for the actions, a day where people will be held accountable for their deeds, it is a day where people will either go to heaven or hell, punished or rewarded, a time that is akin to 50,000 years in this world's terms.
9. She did not want to end up like Dee, die before having accepted the truth, and die a disbeliever
10. It is too late, life on this earth is the only time to submit.
11. It is the truth, Islam is the fastest growing religion, its roots reach far back to the time of Adam, it is a holistic religion, its teachings affecting every aspect of the Muslim's life, Islam holds an authenticity that other religions do not due to the fact that its followers adhere strictly to the original teachings, Islam is the only religion in its orthodox form.

Level II – 6 Essay questions: Each answer is worth 1 to 16 points with a total score of 100 points possible for all five questions

Final Assignment: Assign the students to write a book review for *If I Should Speak*.

If I Should Speak Teacher Study Guide
Author Saba Negash

Saba Negash was born and raised in Southern California. She graduated with a liberal arts degree in 1993 from Victor Valley College and Insha Allah, looks forward to continuing her education in the field of Early Childhood Education. She is from a family of educators. She follows in her mother's footsteps who was an educator and psychologist for over 30 years. Saba enjoys photography, traveling and experiencing new things. Her 15 year teaching career has given her the wonderful opportunity to live and work in many countries. It was through her teaching that she came to love writing curriculum, children's stories, and poems to encourage good morals, character and creativity in her students. Email contact is sabbuha2000@yahoo.com

Saba has authored three teacher study guides for three authors and is published by Muslim Writers Publishing. One of her goals is the promotion of literacy. To support this goal, she created and maintains the *Family Reads Program* that is dedicated to bringing wholesome fun and educational activities that the whole family can enjoy together. Family Reads promotes families reading and learning together. http://familyreads.weebly.com/

If I Should Speak Teacher Study Guide
Content Developer Linda D. Delgado

Linda, known by many as Widad, is a Muslim revert, the mother of three and grandmother of eight. She is a graduate of the University of Phoenix and author of the award winning Islamic Rose Books series. Linda is also the owner-publisher of *Muslim Writers Publishing*.

If I Should Speak novel
Author Umm Zakiyyah

Umm Zakiyyah spent most of her childhood in Indianapolis, Indiana, where she wrote articles for local newspapers and essays and poetry for college publications nationally. In college, as a student at the prestigious Emory University in Atlanta, Georgia, she wrote articles for the school's newspaper and received various awards for her leadership and academic achievements.

In 1997, she graduated from Emory University with a Bachelor of Arts degree in elementary education, and went on to make a name for herself as a writer, teacher, and inspirational speaker. She appeared on radio and TV in the United States and Canada, and was a guest lecturer at national conferences and youth events.

2001 marked the release of Umm Zakiyyah's first novel, *If I Should Speak*. She went on to write *A Voice*, and *Footsteps*, which formed the last two novels in the *If I Should Speak* trilogy. Umm Zakiyyah has written and published two additional novels: *Realities of Submission* and *Hearts We Lost*.

In 2008, she was awarded the Muslim Girls Unity Conference Distinguished Authors Award.
http://www.themuslimauthor.com/

www.ingramcontent.com/pod-product-compliance
Lightning Source LLC
LaVergne TN
LVHW061254060426
835507LV00020B/2317